MW00856244

The Unwanted Undead Adventurer 6 Yu Okano / Illustrator: Jaian

It's hard to describe,
but it looked sinister, to say the least.
It looked like a big, silver wolf, but
its eyes were bloodshot and its
massive body was surrounded by
a wavering wicked black aura.
It appeared to have a thirst for carnage.
It was like destruction incarnate,
or an apostle of Hell.

...shahor melechnamer.

[**sixth** **6**] # The Unwanted Undead Adventurer

Yu Okano
Illustrator: Jaian
Illustration Support: Daisuke Tooya

Clope

Proprietor of the Three-Pronged Harpoon. Produces special weapons and armor that match Rentt's requirements.

Isabel Cariello

Loris's wife. Runs the Red Wyvern Pavilion with him. Business is good.

Loris Cariello

Proprietor of the Red Wyvern Pavilion, a tavern and eatery. Because he was saved by Rentt in the labyrinth, Rentt dines in his tavern for free.

Myullias Raiza

A Saint of the Church of Lobelia. Blessed by the spirits, she is capable of channeling divinity. Wields the powers of healing and purification.

Nive Maris

A Gold-class adventurer, as well as a vampire hunter. She is seen by many as the closest individual to Platinum-class.

Luka

Clope's Wife. Assists him in the daily operations of the Three-Pronged Harpoon.

Story

Rentt, the eternal Bronze-class adventurer, became undead after being eaten by a dragon. Recalling that monsters have the capacity for something called Existential Evolution, he used it to successfully evolve into a ghoul. With the help of Rina, he returned to Maalt and ended up living with Lorraine. Going by an alias, he once again resumed his quest to become a Mithril-class adventurer. However, some time after evolving into a lesser vampire, Rentt had to reveal his true identity to Guildmaster Wolf Hermann in order to resolve the problem with his double registration. Then he and Lorraine traveled to his hometown, the village of Hathara…

Characters

Sheila Ibarss

Receptionist at the adventurer's guild. Knows Rentt's secret.

Lorraine Vivie

Scholar and Silver-class adventurer. Has been offering her support to Rentt ever since he became an undead.

Rentt Faina

An adventurer aspiring to reach Mithril-class. Became an undead after he was consumed by a dragon in the labyrinth.

Edel

A monster commonly referred to as a puchi suri. Became Rentt's familiar after sucking his blood in the basement of Maalt's Second Orphanage.

Alize

A young girl living at the orphanage. Dreams of becoming an adventurer. Currently Lorraine and Rentt's disciple.

Rina Rupaage

A new adventurer who helped Rentt sneak into Maalt after he had evolved into a ghoul.

Idoles Rogue

A knight belonging to the First Brigade of the Kingdom of Yaaran. Has a younger sister by the name of Rina.

Isaac Hart

A servant of the Latuule family. Is capable enough to take on the Tarasque Swamp on his own.

Laura Latuule

The current head of the Latuule family. Loves collecting magical items of all kinds. Rentt is contracted to periodically deliver Dragon Blood Blossoms to her from the swamp.

THE UNWANTED UNDEAD ADVENTURER: VOLUME 6
By Yu Okano

Translated by Noah Rozenberg
Edited by Suzanne Seals
English Print Cover by Mitach

This book is a work of fiction. Names, characters, places, and incidents are the product of the author's imagination or are used fictitiously. Any resemblance to actual events, locales, or persons, living or dead, is coincidental.

Copyright © 2019 Yu Okano
Illustrations by Jaian
Cover Illustration by Jaian

First published in Japan in 2019 by OVERLAP Inc., Tokyo.
Publication rights for this English edition arranged through OVERLAP Inc., Tokyo.

All rights reserved. In accordance with the U.S. Copyright Act of 1976, the scanning, uploading, and electronic sharing of any part of this book without the permission of the publisher is unlawful piracy and theft of the author's intellectual property.

Find more books like this one at www.j-novel.club!

Managing Director: Samuel Pinansky
Light Novel Line Manager: Chi Tran
Managing Editor: Jan Mitsuko Cash
Managing Translator: Kristi Fernandez
QA Manager: Hannah N. Carter
Marketing Manager: Stephanie Hii
Project Manager: Kristine Johnson

ISBN: 978-1-7183-5745-7
Printed in Korea
First Printing: June 2022
10 9 8 7 6 5 4 3 2 1

[C O N T E N T S]

Chapter 1:   My Hometown of Hathara

In the middle of a wooden fence stood a crude gate. We approached it and met two young men standing guard. They both looked at me as soon as they saw us.

"Halt. What business do you have in Hathara?" one of them asked.

"I'm coming back home. Jal, Dol, don't you recognize me?" I asked and smiled. But the smile was hidden under my mask, so all they saw were my narrowed eyes.

The two youths, a skinny one named Jal and a short one named Dol, stared at me curiously. A few moments later, they opened their eyes wide.

"Wait, Rentt?! Is that you?!" they shouted.

"Yeah, can't you tell?"

"No, you looked more like an ordinary adventurer last time you came," Jal said. "Like a swordsman or something. What's with the sketchy robe and mask?" His brow furrowed as he asked.

"I've been through a lot. Anyway, let me in," I answered, dodging the question. Explaining would be a hassle, and I had no intention of telling them everything.

"Well, I guess that's fine. Wait, who's that?" Dol asked when he noticed Lorraine.

"I'm a fellow adventurer," Lorraine proclaimed. "My name is Lorraine Vivie. I also work as a scholar in Maalt. Nice to meet you." She shook their hands.

They both looked bewildered as they shook back, but a second later they dragged me off to the side and spoke into my ear with a shouting whisper.

"Hey! Who's the hot chick?! Don't tell me you're married! Are you married?!" Jal questioned.

Dol quickly added, "Here to report you got married? Is that why you're back?! This is a big deal. We have to tell the mayor!" he said and ran off into the village.

"Hey, wait! You've got it all wrong!" I frantically yelled, but it was too late. Typical of villagers from deep in the mountains, Dol had strong legs and ran fast. It only took a moment before he was out of sight.

"Who would've thought that one of the least sociable people in the village would come back with a wife. Riri and Fahri aren't gonna be happy about this. At least this gives us a chance with them, though," Jal muttered.

Riri and Fahri were considered to be among the most beautiful women in the village. They were also childhood friends of mine, but they were around seven years my junior, so I thought of them like younger sisters. Though it was different in the city, by the village's standards they were getting a bit old for single women. It was a little worrisome. Still, they were gorgeous enough to get married right away if they ever felt like it, so maybe it wasn't worth being concerned about.

In any case, I didn't know why Jal brought them up. "What do you mean, this gives you a chance with them?" I asked.

"I can't believe you," Jal said, appalled. "They were always into you. Didn't they come on to you a few times? And you turned them down."

"Pretty sure it wasn't serious. They did that all the time."

"They gave you honey sweets every year on Saint Alto's Day, didn't they? And they always invited you to the lake during the Nameless Festival," he retorted.

Both of those events were famously meant for couples. The former was celebrated around the world, while the latter was specific to our village. They were embedded enough in our public consciousness that I knew all about them. On Saint Alto's Day, you gave honey sweets to someone you liked. It was also one of the only times of year where it was considered appropriate for a woman to confess her love to a man. As for the Nameless Festival, it had been held in Hathara for so long that even its original name was forgotten. There was a story that went along with it, and the festival was based around that. The story was about a couple that went to a lake, where their love was finally fully realized.

I did receive sweets and get invited to the lake on those holidays, but I left the village shortly before I turned fifteen. At the time, I didn't know how I was supposed to take these approaches from seven- or eight-year-old girls. That hardly seemed like a reason to treat me as unreceptive to their love, though.

On the occasions that I did come back to the village, I was surprised to see how beautiful they had become. And they did similar things during those visits. Regardless, I had known them ever since they were young, so they still felt like precious little sisters to me. And if they looked up to me like a big brother, that wouldn't be especially strange.

"They said they had nobody else and picked me so they could at least experience the holiday," I explained. That must have been where Jal got the wrong idea. They were clearly too young. I didn't have anything against an age gap in relationships between adults, but when you've known someone since they were an infant, it's hard to view them as a member of the opposite sex. I assumed they saw me the same way.

"And you just took that at face value?" Jal spat. "Well, whatever. You brought your wife here, so that's the end of that. Now the village guys can go after Riri and Fahri."

That must have been what he meant by getting a chance. Well, whether they were kidding or not, I didn't have romantic feelings for them. Not that I was married to Lorraine either, but it didn't look like Jal or Dol would listen even if I told them that. Considering Riri and Fahri, maybe this was a convenient misunderstanding, so I didn't want to go out of my way to correct them.

"What are you chatting about? Anything interesting?" Lorraine asked.

She had popped in from behind us, startling Jal. However, I realized she was there from the moment she approached. It would have been different had she used magic to conceal herself, but I could otherwise detect her without any issues. That wasn't the case for Jal.

"Not really," he said. "Well, anyway, no reason to stand around out here. How about we go inside the village? There are some people who'd like to say hi."

"Oh, right," Lorraine replied. "Jal, was it?"

"Yeah, what's up?"

"I know Rentt is allowed in, but am I?" she asked. It should have been fine as long as she was accompanying me, but it was typical of her to ask and make sure.

"Yeah, no problem. You're Rentt's, well, y'know."

"I'm not sure I know, but I'm glad to hear it's fine. Let's go, Rentt," Lorraine said and walked on ahead.

"All right, Jal, we'll be going. See you later," I told him and then waved and followed after Lorraine. We entered the village together.

"Getting dragged around by the wife already, eh? City girls are rough," I heard Jal whisper from behind us. Maybe I was imagining it.

Hathara seldom saw visitors, so I didn't know how they would react to Lorraine, but the villagers we encountered tended to be positive. Just about everyone responded like Jal and Dol. They kept asking if Lorraine was my wife, but at least they did so pleasantly enough. Unlike Jal and Dol, the other villagers had a bit more discretion and listened when I told them she wasn't. They were all smiling a strange amount, but I wanted to believe there was no special reason for that.

"What does this village produce? Is it all farmers and hunters?" Lorraine asked as she observed her surroundings.

"Yeah, for the most part," I answered. "But they grow more than just wheat and vegetables. There's a medicinal herb garden as well, so maybe that's a bit unique."

"A medicinal herb garden? Do they sell the herbs to a bigger town or some merchant or what?"

"I think I've told you about the medicine woman we have here. She uses the herbs to produce medicine, and then she sells that to traveling merchants. It's highly effective and goes for a high price, apparently. Thanks to that, it's not so bad living in this town in the middle of nowhere. They hunt monsters on occasion too, so they also sell magic crystals."

"I always wondered why you were so accustomed to adventurer work from the start. You were already working like an adventurer in this village, from the sound of it."

"Well, pretty much. I helped out with dissecting the monsters a lot, and I naturally picked up on how to walk through forests. Oh hey, that's the mayor's house."

I looked ahead and saw a house one size larger than all the ones around it. We headed toward it. When visiting villages like this, it was customary to greet the mayor first.

That wasn't the only reason I was going there, but it was a good excuse.

I knocked on the door, and it slowly opened. A middle-aged woman peeked out from the other side. It had been a while since I'd seen her face; she had visibly aged, but she was still slender and beautiful. When she saw me, she opened her eyes wide. A few tears slipped out.

"Rentt, good to see you're back. I was worried about you. When the guild told me you'd gone missing, I was sure you'd never return. Thank goodness I was wrong," she cried.

The guild wasn't so kind as to go out of its way to report to an adventurer's hometown when they went missing, but Guildmaster Wolf had probably arranged differently in my case. He now knew that I was alive, but he must not have contacted the village about that yet. Even though there were methods of contact using flying creatures, they didn't use those for backwater towns like this. Carriages were the only option. Maybe the carriage we came in on was carrying a letter like that. But I didn't know if reporting that I was alive would technically be accurate, and maybe Wolf wasn't sure either, so who knows if he thought to send anything yet.

"It's complicated, but as you can see, I'm in pretty good health. By the way, where's Dad?"

"Oh, he's here. Come in and— Oh? Who's this?"

"Lorraine, a friend from Maalt. She's a scholar," I said.

Lorraine looked like she had a lot to say about that but decided it was best to hold it back. "I'm Lorraine Vivie. I'm a scholar, like Rentt said, as well as an adventurer, and I also dabble in alchemy. Pleased to meet you. And you are?"

"A scholar? Interesting. I'm sorry I didn't introduce myself sooner. I'm Gilda Faina, the wife of the mayor, Ingo Faina. It's nice to meet you too."

"Faina?" Lorraine repeated with shock. "Don't tell me you're Rentt's—"

"Yeah, she's my mom. The mayor's my dad. And that medicine woman I talked about would be my grandmother's younger sister, if I'm remembering that right."

"I wasn't expecting you to bring a woman home to the village. Not that I'm complaining. I'm glad to see it, actually," Ingo said.

He was sitting at the table, so we all decided to take a seat as well. Once everyone introduced themselves, we started to chat. It was mostly one-sided, with Lorraine and I telling them what I had been up to in Maalt. In return, Ingo and Gilda had a bit to say about the goings-on in the village.

One topic of discussion was all the villagers who were starting to get married. They said that most of the children I looked after back in the day had significant others now. A fair number of them even had children of they're own. When I came to visit over a year ago, there did seem to be a lot of people getting friendly with each other. That must have been the season of love.

Now that I thought about it, there were quite a few people around my age who got married two or three years after I left the village. Sometimes I saw their children running around like I used to do. It made me feel like I had taken an unusual course in life. I did feel a bit lonely, but more than that, I was happy to see the village doing well.

Around the time we began to discuss marriage, Ingo and Gilda started to look at Lorraine a bit differently.

"Yes, you always stuck to your training no matter who asked you out. I was afraid you'd never get married. At least it's nice to see you found such a pretty girl outside the village," Gilda said.

I wasn't always the most perceptive person, but even I saw what she was getting at. She assumed Lorraine was my wife. But the women of this village were masters of conversation and knew how to dance around the subject. She just wanted me to confirm or deny it without asking directly. Maybe she was being considerate, in a sense, but it also felt like I had to walk on a bed of nails.

Unlike me, Lorraine wasn't nervous at all. In fact, she was calm and collected. "Rentt has quite a number of female acquaintances in Maalt," she said. "There's Rina, Sheila, me, Lillian, Alize... I could go on..."

The way she listed them off sounded malicious. Simply stating their names made it easy to imagine they were all beautiful women of marriageable age, but Rina was even more like a little sister to me than Riri or Fahri were, and Lillian was far older than me. And then there was Alize, a child by any metric. Sheila was, I suppose, a woman of an appropriate age, but I only knew her through work. We were connected by circumstance, but that was all. That's how I saw it, at least.

As for Lorraine, though, the fact that I lived with her made it hard to argue with how the villagers saw our relationship. But in Maalt, plenty of adventurers of opposite genders lived together in the same house. It wasn't that big of a deal. Probably. Maybe it was just me. Either way, Lorraine, Ingo, and Gilda didn't give me the opportunity to say any of this.

"Oh my, he knows all these women? Then I suppose I was worried for nothing. I wasn't kidding when I said I thought he might never get married."

"Really? I know he can be socially inept, but certainly women approach him a fair bit. I don't see him as the type to stubbornly reject them all, either."

"Sounds like you know Rentt well. That's true, but nobody in this village was ever able to go this far with him."

"What?" Lorraine asked and cocked her head, but her question was brushed aside.

"Oh, right, now that Rentt's back, I think the village should hold a welcoming banquet. Could you make the preparations, Gilda?"

"Yes, of course, dear. Enjoy yourselves, you two. I'll go tell the villagers," Gilda said as she stood and exited the house.

"I'll be going too," Ingo informed us just as she left. "It's a small village, but we have a decent number of citizens. Gilda might find it hard to tell everyone by herself." He followed Gilda out the door.

Lorraine watched them go. "Hey, Rentt," she whispered.

"What?"

"Did I say something I shouldn't have?"

"No, not at all. I'm the problem here. They worry about me so much that it's kind of unbearable."

"Why do you feel that way?"

"Well, they're not my birth parents, but they adopted me."

"You were adopted? What happened to your birth parents?" Lorraine asked.

Lorraine didn't beat around the bush, even with a difficult question. I knew she wasn't trying to be insensitive; Lorraine just had a tendency to be direct. If I said I didn't want to talk about it, she would likely drop the subject and move on. In other words, while she had asked about it, it was only to give me the option of whether to discuss it or not.

It wasn't something I was that adamant about avoiding, so I went ahead and told her. "They died a long time ago. I was five when it happened," I explained.

It was the simple truth, and talking about it didn't hurt too much anymore. Regardless, it would always be sad. I never forgot their faces, and I would always remember our life together. They were good people. I wished they could still be alive, but it wasn't to be.

"I see. Were they ill?"

"Attacked by monsters. It happens all the time," I said, trying not to sound too serious, but I noticed I sounded shaky.

When I became undead, I started to think my body couldn't produce tears anymore. As it turned out, that wasn't the case. When I checked my eyes in the mirror, they were as moist as any human eyes. I supposed there was no reason I wouldn't be able to cry. Now I felt like I could tear up at any moment.

"Is that why you wanted to be an adventurer?"

"Well, for the most part. That wasn't the only reason, though. Anyway, when I told my adoptive parents what I wanted to do, they were pretty supportive. Actually, sorry, Lorraine, but I'm going out for a bit too. Do you mind waiting in this house for a little while? I'm sure it won't be too comfy sitting around in someone else's house."

"Hm? Oh, I don't mind if you don't. You want me to watch your family's house?"

"I'd trust you to do it more than anyone. See you later," I said and left the house.

I knew it wasn't the best thing to do, but if I stayed any longer, I might have started sobbing. That would only bother Lorraine. In the decade I'd known her, I never once cried in front of her. Actually, maybe I had, now that I thought about it, but it didn't need to happen again. It was an issue of my meager male pride. I'd take a little walk around the village and give my eyes a chance to dry, then I'd go back. I didn't want to keep her waiting too long.

Sinking into a chair at the mayor's house, Lorraine felt as if she had stomped on a landmine. She had gone too far with what she'd said to Rentt's parents. However, while some frivolous conversation might have been preferable if this were a simple visit to Rentt's hometown, she wanted it to be more than that.

Some part of Lorraine was curious to learn about Rentt's past, and maybe that part of her controlled her actions more than she cared to realize. She wanted to believe it was a desire driven by her researcher's spirit, but she suspected it had more to do with her personal feelings.

They had been friends for a decade, but they always kept a certain amount of distance. It was pleasant in a way that her life in Lelmudan never was. She did have friends in her home country, of course, but Lorraine held a special position there. She was never able to develop a relationship as naturally as she could with Rentt. That was why her feelings for Rentt were so strong...

and even dependent in some respects. She had no intention of relying on him to excess, but without him, she would feel hopeless.

Lorraine was keenly aware of what Rentt meant to her. If she had to name the feeling, she knew what she would call it. But she had to put that aside for now. She knew thinking about it too much wouldn't lead anywhere good.

Regardless, she thought back to everything she had just heard. The fact that Rentt's parents were the mayor and his wife was surprising enough, but she hadn't expected him to be adopted too. When there were orphans in villages this small, it was common for the mayor to take them in. That part wasn't unusual, but Lorraine had never imagined it had happened to Rentt. In some ways it made sense, and in others it was unbelievable.

Considering Rentt's personality, this came as a shock to her. He was always carefree, for better or worse, and never seemed to mind much. That was a trait only someone who had the chance to grow up comfortably from the day they became self-aware could develop. When children lost their parents and got taken in by another family, they tended to develop more timid personalities. Since Rentt managed to grow up the way he did, the mayor and his wife must have been good parents.

This discovery did explain, however, why Rentt was oddly multi-talented for someone from a small village. He could write and make medicine; he had formal training in combat; and he was strangely dexterous. As the mayor's son, he would have received a fair bit of education, explaining his skills to an extent. Even so, his abilities seemed better than they should have been. Maybe that was thanks to all the hard work he put in to become an adventurer.

If his desire to become an adventurer stemmed from monsters killing his parents, maybe he was out for revenge... But that didn't sound quite right to Lorraine. He said he had other reasons too. Knowing Rentt, he wouldn't be driven by revenge so much as a desire to prevent the sort of sorrow he'd had to experience. The conversation had ended before she could ask about it, but judging by Rentt's actions in Maalt, she believed she was right. His efforts to reduce the death rate of new adventurers reflected that.

She could ask more about it once Rentt returned, but she wasn't sure how she should ask. If she wasn't cautious, she might step on another landmine. At least if it made him openly angry, she wouldn't mind, but he always tried to pretend that he didn't mind at all. It hurt her to see him like that. "What to do?" Lorraine muttered to herself.

There was a knock at the door. It was likely a visitor, but Lorraine didn't live in this house and wasn't sure if answering the door was the best idea. She considered pretending nobody was home, but she had just walked through the village, so enough people knew about her. She didn't need to be so cautious, though, and she didn't want to pretend she wasn't around. If anything, that would make her look more suspicious.

That being the case, there was only one thing to do. Lorraine stood up and headed to the door.

"Oh, Rentt, are you here? Wait, no?"

"Ren? Or, um, who are you?"

Two girls were at the door. One had a firm, clear voice, while the other had a gentle, sweet tone. Lorraine figured these voices could only belong to young girls.

When they saw Lorraine's face, they fell silent. This was, of course, because neither Rentt nor his family were at home, but someone unknown had answered the door. Lorraine had no idea who these girls were either, so she didn't know what to say. The tension stretched into awkwardness.

Lorraine was the adult in this situation, so she was able to pull herself together quicker. "Sorry, but Rentt and his parents are away at the moment," she offered. "They asked me to look after the house. I'm Lorraine Vivie, Rentt's, uh, friend." She wasn't sure how to treat the girls, but they had spoken frankly to her, so she didn't see the need to be overly polite.

"Rentt's friend?" one of the girls repeated. She had brown pigtails and bold eyes. "Oh, right, I heard he had a scholar friend in the city. But you're a woman?!"

"Now that you mention it, he never said whether they were a man or a woman," the other girl said. She had bluish-black hair that only went down to her ears and soft eyes. "But still, wow, Riri, she's pretty hot. And kind of cool, too. I bet cities have lots of people like this."

"Fahri! How can you be so calm?! From what I heard from Auntie, Rentt's been living with this person! Even Rentt couldn't resist a girl like this!"

"It does seem like it'd be hard. I'd like to touch her in a few places myself. I wonder if she'd go for it," Fahri said. She reached a hand toward Lorraine, seemingly toward her chest.

Lorraine didn't know what to make of these two. "Should I assume you're friends of Rentt?"

"Yep, you got it," one of them answered, a sharp look in her eyes. "I'm Riri. This sleepy-looking girl is—"

"Fahri. Nice to meet you."

"All right, then," Lorraine said. "Nice to meet you, too. Anyway, I'd invite you to come in, but this isn't my house. They trusted me to watch the place, so I can't just let anyone inside. If you have business with Rentt's family, I'm sure they'll be back soon enough, so maybe you could come back later." Of course, if they knew Rentt, then it would probably be fine to allow them inside, but Lorraine didn't want to make assumptions.

"Hm, I guess that makes sense," Riri replied. "We pretty much welcome any visitors around here, but maybe that's different in the city."

"Well, yes," Lorraine answered. "We get a fair number of thieves. If you walk around town a bit, you're bound to run into at least one pickpocket."

Riri laughed and looked at Fahri. "Wow, sounds dangerous. Fahri wouldn't make it through a day without going broke."

Fahri pouted. "I'd just have to be careful, then I'd be fine. Maybe." She didn't seem like she'd be fine at all.

"The city, huh? I've never been outside the village, personally," Riri admitted. "I've always wondered what it's like. What about you, Fahri?"

"I'm curious too. I've gotten souvenirs from people who left the village, but that's about it."

Riri nodded and looked back at Lorraine. "Yeah, so, Lorraine?"

"What?" Lorraine asked and cocked her head.

"We get that Rentt's out. I mean, we knew his parents were away before we came. We just ran into Auntie, and she said that Rentt's here. That's all fine, but we'd like to speak with you for a bit. We've barely seen anything outside the village, so it'd be nice to hear about the big city."

By the big city, presumably they meant Maalt. The Lelmudan Empire was even more urban, so Lorraine didn't think of Maalt that way, but it was certainly a bigger city than this village. She'd heard plenty from Rentt about how small his village was, but she'd never imagined just how small. Similarly, these girls didn't have much of an understanding of what big cities were like.

"I can tell you, but I'm still not going to let you in the house. You may think that's stubborn of me, but it's how I am," Lorraine said. She could often be negligent, but she was persistent when she wanted to be. When it came to academics, for example, she was meticulous. She always tried to do what seemed sensible to her, as in this occasion. But she did also recognize that she could be inflexible to other perspectives...particularly when it came to this village, where nobody locked their doors or minded any visitors.

"I understand," Riri said. "We can talk right here. Look, here's a perfectly nice place to sit." She pointed to some chairs made out of logs sitting in front of the house. There were around ten of them, most likely there for when work had to be done outside.

While Lorraine had her reservations about letting them inside, Riri was right; chatting outside should be fine. It just came down to whether Lorraine was interested or not.

"Well, I suppose that'll be all right. I'm curious to hear what it's like living in this village as well. Rentt hardly ever talks about his life here."

"Really? Whenever Ren comes to visit, he hardly talks about life in the city," Fahri said, wide-eyed.

Lorraine could immediately guess why Rentt never said anything about Maalt. Even a decade later, Rentt still hadn't risen above Bronze-class. Lorraine didn't think there was anything wrong with that. The fact he'd made it that long without dying or suffering any serious injuries was impressive for an adventurer. But Rentt probably found it hard to return to his hometown with pride. Lorraine knew how that felt. If she was going to talk to Riri and Fahri, she would have to keep that in mind.

Taking that into consideration, she sat in a log chair and faced the two girls.

"So, Ren's been adventuring around Maalt, right? What's that like?" the sleepy girl asked. She was brimming with anticipation, eager to hear about Rentt's glorious accomplishments. Next to her, Riri looked just as curious.

They obviously had great expectations, but Lorraine wasn't sure what to tell them. She would never say that Rentt had accomplished nothing over the last decade, but much of what he had done was rather plain. His main achievements amounted to looking after new adventurers and lowering the adventurer death rate. That was exciting in its own way, but it probably wasn't what a couple of village girls who longed to see the city must have imagined when they thought of adventurers. Lorraine figured it would be best to focus on recent events. As for his rank, she could avoid that subject.

"Well, I think Rentt's a pretty famous adventurer in Maalt. He takes good care of his fellow adventurers, and all the newbies look up to him."

"Huh, so not much has changed for him in the city, from what it sounds like," Riri commented.

"What do you mean?" Lorraine cocked her head.

"Well, when he lived in Hathara, he always looked after the younger kids. It sounds like he's doing the same thing in the city."

29

"Hm, I see."

Rentt's oddly caring personality must have taken shape in this village. Riri and Fahri had most likely been under Rentt's care at some point as well.

"So what about monsters? Beating monsters is an adventurer's main job, right? We have hunters that go after monsters here, but there's supposed to be dungeons around Maalt, and I bet those are full of strong ones," Riri said.

Lorraine thought for a bit. Rentt primarily hunted slimes, goblins, and skeletons, all of which were famously weak monsters. These villagers likely knew as much. Of course, for an ordinary villager, they were still fearsome enough, but in fairy tales and picture books they were always slain as easily as ants. Few people would be intrigued by stories about slaying these monsters. None of them drew much interest aside from slimes, which had some appeal to merchants because they could be made into lotions or potions. Adventurers who could capture tons of slimes were treasured, but these villagers wouldn't know about that.

Lorraine assumed they would be more impressed by tales of slaying giant monsters. Such stories were always entertaining, to the point that when Lorraine had once gone to a bar in a distant village and she'd been asked to tell a story, that was the subject matter she'd picked. Adventurers themselves didn't care much for these stories because they understood the real strength of monsters and recognized that large monsters weren't necessarily powerful, but for common villagers, the bigger the better.

One of Lorraine's go-to stories was when she defeated a grand fum wyvern that was ten meters in length. The giant creature lived near the peak of a mountain, where Lorraine pierced it with dozens of ice spears and severed its head with a wind blade when it fell to the ground. She embellished that story as much as possible, and if she was in a large enough space, she would use projection magic to create an image and display just how large the wyvern was. A three-dimensional projection of a giant wyvern was enough to make villagers tremble, and the idea that Lorraine defeated it by herself made them look at her with awe and respect. They welcomed her after that, bringing her food and drinks at huge discounts, if not offering them for free. That wasn't her goal when she told this story, but it was a nice bonus.

In reality, however, grand fum wyverns were just a flying species of demidragon and the weakest of the zeva wyverns. It had low magic resistance, so for a magician of Lorraine's talent, it was little more than a target to be shot down. Not only that, its size made it easier to hit, and if its dwelling was discovered, magic circles could be set up around it and charged with mana in advance to be triggered when the wyvern took flight. If she were honest, it was a simple monster to defeat. She often felt bad when she boasted about this story, but when she spoke about truly daunting battles with monsters, she often got confused looks. As such, she still felt that tales about hunting large monsters were the best choice.

"Yes, Maalt has dungeons. The Water Moon Dungeon and the New Moon Dungeon, specifically. They have monsters of all sorts. Rentt goes to both dungeons nowadays, though there was a time when he mostly went to the Water Moon Dungeon. There he encountered a monster called a giant skeleton," Lorraine said. She used magic to construct an image of the monster to accompany the story.

"Eep!"

"Wh-What?"

Riri and Fahri gasped when they saw it. It was massive enough to smash a house, so their shock was to be expected. Of course, this was merely an image and couldn't do anything, but Lorraine feared that its sudden appearance might startle other villagers, so she limited who could see it. It was only visible to Riri, Fahri, and herself.

"No need to worry, this is just an illusion," Lorraine explained.

"B-B-But I see it right there!"

"Y-Yeah."

They didn't seem to believe it, but Lorraine knew how they felt. This was like nothing that mountain villagers would have ever seen before. Not many people could use this projection spell. Lorraine was able to use it freely, but it was actually a difficult spell to control. Casting it in Maalt would receive a similar reaction, so Lorraine did her part to demonstrate that it was safe by making the illusion move and touch her.

"See? It's fine," she said and touched the giant skeleton. Her hand went right through it. She pulled her hand back out to show that it was still there. When Riri and Fahri saw this, they seemed relieved.

"You're right, nothing happens when I touch it."

"It's so weird, huh, Riri? Is this magic?" Fahri wondered.

"Yes, it is. Do you not have any sorcerers in this village?" Lorraine asked. The reality was there were few sorcerers in general. Even simple life magic spells were inaccessible to the majority of the population. But even in this small village, statistically speaking, there had to be at least one person with mana. They would still have to know how to use their mana to cast spells, however.

"There's a medicine woman named Gharb who can use alchemy, so I guess she can use magic," Fahri answered. "But she never uses it in public. I've never seen magic like this before."

That must have been the medicine woman Rentt talked about. He said that her medicine was unusually good for an average villager, but if she could use alchemy, then that explained it. Rentt never mentioned that, though, so Lorraine was still left with questions.

"Wait, Fahri, I never knew that," Riri said. "Gharb's a sorcerer?"

Fahri looked like she regretted bringing it up, but she saw no use hiding it now. "Yeah, she is. That was supposed to be a secret, though."

"A secret? Why?" Riri asked.

"When you live in a small village, it's not good to tell people you can use magic."

"You sure didn't have any problems saying it, Fahri."

"Well, only because Lorraine uses magic. Gharb said magicians can identify magicians, so there's no use trying to hide it from them," Fahri said.

Lorraine could confirm that she was correct. Normal people had no easy way to tell, but if a sorcerer paid attention, they could tell whether someone had mana. Only special people like Lorraine could tell by sight, but most sorcerers knew how to sense magic energy. Regardless, it took some practice to get it right all the time, so it wasn't something everyone could do, but it was safest to assume that sorcerers had this ability.

"Fahri, you seem to have some mana as well," Lorraine noted. "Does that have something to do with how you knew she was a magician?"

"Yes. Gharb was teaching me to make medicine, and apparently I have a bit of mana, so she said she'd teach me alchemy too at some point."

"I see."

That meant she still hadn't been taught yet. Unlike Lorraine's attempts to almost force Alize to become aware of her mana, Gharb must have been taking her time with Fahri. Lorraine did things her own way, but her methods could be fairly dangerous with a less skilled teacher, potentially leading to the student's death. The standard method was to do nothing more than let a little mana flow each day, and do this every day for weeks on end. That was presumably Gharb's approach, and it signaled that she took good care of her students.

"No fair, Fahri. I want to learn magic so I can do stuff like this!" Riri pouted and pointed to the image of the giant skeleton.

Fahri wasn't particularly intimidated. "Riri, you're learning something from Hadeed the hunter, aren't you?" she asked calmly. "Just the other day, I saw you cutting logs in the forest with a dagger. You can also shoot arrows insanely far."

"You saw that?" Riri asked, her eyes wide with shock.

Lorraine had an idea as to what Fahri was talking about. "So you have spirit, I take it. I'm no expert on the subject, but I believe it lets you do some interesting things," Lorraine said.

Rentt had some related skills as well, but she didn't know where he'd learned them. It seemed they were commonplace in his village, but these weren't such simple abilities that the average mountain village would have them, so naturally she had questions. The idea that a talented fighter retired to live in a small village and passed down their techniques wasn't inconceivable, but a lot about this village seemed extraordinary. Maybe that explained how they were able to live normal lives so high in the mountains.

"How do you know that?" Riri asked, stunned.

As had occurred to Lorraine many times throughout their conversation, this girl did a poor job of hiding her feelings. In contrast, Fahri always had a soft smile on her face, but it could be hard to get a read on her. Lorraine suspected that she wasn't to be underestimated.

"I'm not an adventurer for nothing," Lorraine said. "I know a number of spirit users. Actually, I never mentioned that, did I?" When she'd introduced herself, she only mentioned being a friend of Rentt, and Riri said she'd heard Lorraine was a scholar, but that was all.

"No, I thought you were just a scholar."

"I'm a scholar, a magician, and an alchemist. Maybe it would be best to focus on one thing, but I have many interests. You only live once, so I intend to do everything I want to do."

For most people, dabbling in so many fields would leave their skills half-baked in at least one area, but Lorraine was top-rate at all of them. That couldn't easily be explained by her many-faceted interests, but these girls didn't know the circumstances around that. They were simply impressed.

"So that's how you could tell I had spirit?"

"Well, more or less. Unfortunately, I can't use spirit, though."

Rentt was a spirit user, so she did know plenty about it. She had seen him use it numerous times, and she understood the nature of it to some extent. She had considered practicing with spirit in the past, but as far as she heard from Rentt about his practicing methods, it was hard on the body and wouldn't be suitable for her.

"But you girls are pretty remarkable. A magician and a hunter with the power of spirit? Once you get a little experience, you could probably be adventurers," Lorraine said. They had the talent for it, at least. Experience could come from simply slaying monsters in the area.

Adventurers seldom came from small villages, but this one had produced Rentt, and these two girls had potential too. Lorraine couldn't stop thinking about how strange this village was.

"Really? I hear it's tough being an adventurer, though," Riri said, leaning forward in her chair. She seemed not only interested in Rentt but in adventurers as a whole.

As the one with the knowledge, Lorraine didn't want to mislead them, so she provided a serious answer. "Yes, it does have its challenging aspects, and I don't just mean monsters. Adventuring as a profession demands a wide array of knowledge and experience, not to mention strong mental fortitude," she explained, looking at Riri and Fahri's faces.

Lorraine feared she may have been a bit abstract, judging by their confusion, so she went on. "For example, say you take a job to collect herbs for the purpose of making medicine. There are quite a few jobs of this nature. I take them, and Rentt often does as well, but they do require proper preparation. Young and inexperienced adventurers tend to think these jobs are extremely simple, but they're not."

"Why's that? If you know where the herbs grow, I'd think you could just go pick them without fighting any monsters," Fahri said.

"That's true," Lorraine acknowledged, though she also shook her head. "But in reality, there's a reason it's difficult. First of all, you have to actually know the properties of these plants to have any success locating them. If not, you could easily wander the forest for a whole day and find nothing. That tends to happen to newbies. They can even take the wrong jobs at times. The guild's laziness is partially to blame for that, though. Of course, the plants you can find will change depending on the season. Sometimes, requests to collect plants that don't grow in the current season will be left up on the request board. If you take one of those jobs without realizing this, you may end up having to pay a penalty later."

As to why these jobs remained on the board, there were a number of reasons. It was partially malicious, serving as a way to collect penalty payments from new and ignorant adventurers. Maalt's guild was generous enough that it usually did remove these postings when the time came, but most guilds left the selection of jobs to the adventurers, so discretion was required. Even in Maalt, there were occasions where off-season jobs remained posted. If someone wanted certain plants that weren't available that season for whatever reason, they might post a job with a considerably higher-than-average reward. Under these circumstances, Maalt would leave the job up, and the nature of the request would be clear after talking to guild staff. However, newbies just assumed they were simple jobs with strangely high rewards and thought they got lucky to find them. The end result was that they had to pay a penalty fee. To avoid this, adventurers needed knowledge and experience.

"And even if you do happen to get lucky and find the plants, that's not enough," Lorraine continued.

"Can't you just pull them up or dig them out or whatever and take them back to town?" Riri asked.

"Not necessarily," Lorraine said and shook her head. "Plants are living things and must be delivered safely if you want the guild to accept them. You could end up toiling all day only to make not even a single coin."

"Oh, and depending on what the plants are meant to be used for, you have to pick them differently. I know about that," Fahri declared. While Riri didn't seem to understand, Fahri had learned about herbs from the medicine woman.

"That's right," Lorraine said. "For example, if the request demands the roots be intact, you have to uproot the entire plant. That means you need to dig up the dirt around it and wrap it in cloth to keep it safe. Whereas if they only request the leaves but demand they be delivered fresh, then they may wither on the way back if you try to take the entire plant. The proper approach for that job would be to only take the leaves. Other matters to consider are the way in which you cut the branches and pick the fruit, the time frame at which the flowers bloom, and more. Even when it comes to picking plants, there's a lot to remember."

Lorraine had first learned all of this from Rentt. She'd studied books and possessed a lot of knowledge as a result, but she'd put little of it into practice, so as she walked through the forest with Rentt, she gained some experience. Much of what the world had to offer needed to be tried to be understood. Her experiences from those moments remained with her to this day and proved helpful to her scholarly work. Rentt had also likely learned from the same medicine woman as Fahri, meaning that in some sense, Lorraine and Fahri's knowledge stemmed from the same source. Lorraine decided that she would have to introduce herself to the medicine woman at some point.

"Well, that's the general idea. Monsters aren't the only trouble an adventurer has to go through. Even so, I won't deny that creatures like these are the greatest danger," Lorraine said and pointed to the figure of the giant skeleton behind her. Its eye sockets paid no attention to them, but its mere presence was terrifying. If a real giant skeleton were to go on a rampage through the village, they could only imagine how dangerous it would be. To Riri and Fahri, even this illusion brought horrors to mind.

"Rentt fights monsters like these every day?" Riri whispered with shock and awe.

Lorraine could have said these types of monsters were extremely rare and only encountered if one was unlucky, but that wouldn't be the best response for Rentt's reputation.

"Yes, yes he does. And he always wins. He's incredible," Lorraine claimed.

If Rentt were here, he would no doubt deny it and point out that this obviously wasn't an everyday occurrence. If he counted the times he fled from such monsters, there would be too many instances to list, but thankfully, Rentt wasn't present. Lorraine was free to stretch the truth a little. Either way, Rentt was now probably strong enough to fight giant skeletons every day and live to tell the tale. He was powerful enough to hunt tarasques, after all.

With that in mind, Lorraine projected an illusion of another monster.

"Rentt also fights monsters like these," she said. She dropped the image of the giant skeleton, replacing it with the massive figure of a tarasque.

Riri and Fahri looked at the monster Lorraine had conjured and whispered to each other.

"What's this?"

"It's kind of like a turtle, but with a long neck and scales. Is it a dragon?"

"No, this is a variety of demidragon," Lorraine responded. "But you have to be at least a Gold-class adventurer to take one on. They have hard shells, six legs, and thick scales that can deflect arrows. But their most dangerous trait is that they spit poison, not to mention their poisonous flesh and blood. Their presence alone can turn their surroundings into a lethal swamp, creating a haven for creatures who dwell in toxicity."

That was how the Swamp of Tarasque came to be. The creatures that lived there had all developed a resistance to tarasque poison in some way or another. It was hard to see how anything could survive there, but life-forms could often be mysterious, and some would inevitably acclimate to such environments over time.

Adventurers, however, preferred to avoid the place. Tarasque poison was powerful enough to kill an ordinary human within minutes. Unfortunately, it was the only place to collect a special flower known as the Dragon Blood Blossom. Adventurers sometimes had no choice but to visit the swamp; it was just one of the many challenges of the job. Since poison now had no effect on him, Rentt had it easy in that regard. Lorraine would love to have that same ability, but it wasn't so easily attained. It wasn't as if she could find the same dragon and let it eat her too.

"Ren slayed one of these, right?" Fahri asked.

"Yes, he hunts these periodically. Their scales and shells are used for weapons and armor, so they sell for a fine price."

"What?! But aren't they poisonous? How does he hunt them?" Riri immediately questioned.

It occurred to Lorraine that she couldn't answer honestly, so instead she told them how adventurers usually handled it. "They are poisonous, yes, but there are various ways to get around that. Otherwise they would be impossible to hunt. You can douse yourself in powerful holy water, or you can equip magic items that resist or nullify poison. There are other methods as well. Rentt hasn't told me precisely what he does, but he always makes it back unharmed, so I assume he takes the proper countermeasures."

The truth was that poison simply had no effect on him as an undead. But no human was entirely immune to poison. Specially trained assassins were an exception, but Rentt was no assassin. His mask and robe might make him look like one, though.

"That's good to hear," Riri said with relief. "Rentt does some crazy things sometimes."

"Does he? He does at times appear to act without thinking, but I think he actually takes a lot into consideration," Lorraine replied.

He did seem to space out quite a bit, but when he came to a decision, he could be frightfully crafty. Rentt was only Bronze-class, but he still gave lectures and advice to newcomers, even the ones who looked down on him for his rank. If they ever tried to antagonize him, he would begin by reacting peacefully. If they forced his hand, however, he could ruin their life. He wouldn't kill them or break their limbs or anything, but he could make sure they never got work as an adventurer. Or he could make it hard for them to live in Maalt. If Rentt ever decided to make a living on dastardly plots, he would likely accomplish some unbelievable feats. But he wouldn't do that.

"Well, that's true," Riri said. "But a long time ago, when a kid went into the forest without an adult's permission, Rentt went after them by himself and fought off monsters to bring them back. Even though he was just a kid too."

"Oh, I remember that," Fahri added. "All the adults who could hunt were out exterminating a goblin dwelling at the time, I think."

"Yeah, that was it. So, Rentt said he'd go find them all on his own. Then he came back covered in blood. I thought I might die of shock."

Lorraine furrowed her brow. "He's always been that ridiculous?"

Rentt generally made plans in advance and acted with efficiency, but when a life was in danger and he believed sacrificing himself could help, he was willing to put his own life on the line. Typically, when village children got lost, either an adult would go find them or, if there was no sign of the child, they would give up and abandon them. It was easy to imagine that Rentt refused to let that happen. Still, it was an absurd action to take.

"Well, he doesn't do anything that crazy anymore. Maybe. Not when it comes to monsters, at least," Lorraine said, thinking about the situation with Nive Maris. At the very least, Rentt could now compete with any monsters on the lower levels of a dungeon. Monsters like earth dragons were still out of the question, but that was true for any average adventurer. In any event, they were seldom encountered.

"Is Rentt that strong?" Riri asked, not noticing the implicit meaning of Lorraine's words.

Rather than answering, Lorraine conjured an image of Rentt in front of the tarasque illusion.

Riri and Fahri both shouted in surprise.

"Rentt?!"

"Ren?!"

"He's just an illusion," Lorraine explained. "I figured I would recreate the battle between Rentt and the tarasque, if you'd like to see it." Lorraine hadn't seen it happen herself, but she'd heard the story from Rentt. She'd also fought tarasques herself, so she could imagine what it was like.

Riri and Fahri both nodded.

"I'd love to see it!"

"If you can show us, please do."

A small, robed man ran toward a monster more massive than most people would ever see in their lifetime. An eerie, skull-shaped mask covered the lower half of his face and hid his expression, but there was a sharp look in his eyes. Though it was deadly, he confronted the poison-spitting tarasque without a sliver of fear.

He approached and drew his sword as if this were a daily occurrence. The tarasque let out an ear-piercing scream, but the man was unaffected. His courage and determination were awe-inspiring. After all, if he hadn't believed he could defeat this unparalleled monstrosity, he would have reacted to the devastating roar in some way.

The man's confidence wasn't the product of inexperience. It was the result of accurate judgment honed through endless training.

As soon as the man reached the tarasque, he leaped and targeted its neck with his sword. The sword itself wasn't particularly remarkable; it lacked luster. But while it wasn't anything special, it was a solid piece of work. All the man wanted was a weapon he could trust with his life, and this blade fulfilled that desire.

As he swung, he applied spirit energy to the blade, giving it a faint glow. Thoroughly condensed spirit energy was said to be strong enough to destroy armaments, and this energy could snap any average sword in half. However, no such damage occurred to this weapon because a master craftsman had created it. As he watched the blade descend, he felt renewed appreciation for its artistry.

He swung the shimmering blade down upon the tarasque's neck, but it bounced off the beast's scales. Some scales peeled off, but the flesh underneath remained undamaged. The tarasque lived up to its reputation. It was clearly a force to be reckoned with from the start.

The reality of the perilous situation struck him. Even so, he refused to let fear engulf him. He would not give up on the challenge. In fact, he was delighted to discover that this monster was tougher than expected.

He gave the tarasque a sharp look, analyzing where to attack next. It seemed best to strike the neck again; it was only a split-second decision but likely the correct one. Some of the scales were detached by his last attack, so if he targeted the same spot again, he wouldn't have to contend with its natural armor. This time, the man's spirit strike would connect.

However, the tarasque understood the man's objective. It turned back toward him, glaring. It had no intention of letting another attack land. Then, without warning, it opened its mouth. The man paused, wondering what was happening, and the tarasque blew purple breath at him. It was poison, the tarasque's specialty, and it was strong enough to melt a man down to the bone within seconds. The man, like any other human, was not immune to poison. If he hadn't already thought this through before he came to fight the tarasque, this would have meant death.

At some point, the man began to emit a blue glow. It was the sacred light of holy water, which he had doused himself with in advance. Even the tarasque's mighty poison was powerless before the protection of God. He ran through the purple breath as if it were merely rain. The tarasque began backing away, as if intimidated, but it couldn't accept that this puny human was a threat. It stopped its retreat and then continued to exhale poison as it marched forward.

The tarasque's sheer size was destructive enough, but the man was unfazed. In fact, he was so casual about it that he looked like he could start whistling at any moment. Its poison had no effect, and its size didn't scare him. Rather, the bigger it was, the more marks he could hit.

The man boldly waited for the tarasque to close in and then jumped onto its shell. The tarasque lost sight of him and panicked, giving the man a chance to run from the shell onto its long neck. He targeted the same spot his sword struck before. His aim was steady, his eyes locked onto the broken scales. Only then did the tarasque realize what was happening, but it was too late. Before it could shake him off, he jumped and raised his sword over his head.

The tarasque cried out, perhaps to beg for mercy. This was the first time it had been not the hunter but the hunted. This tiny man should have been the prey, but the tarasque was forced to acknowledge it had been overpowered.

The monster's pleading meant nothing to the man, for he was an adventurer. Hunting monsters was how he made his living. Listening to the forlorn cries of monsters would be bad for business. But just before his blade connected with flesh, it sounded like the man apologized. He even seemed to empathize with the monster. Still, he didn't hesitate to cut off the tarasque's head. Seconds later, the tarasque collapsed to the ground with a loud boom. He didn't turn to watch, but the sound conveyed the weight of this severed life.

Lorraine felt her presentation may have been a bit flashy. She had left out Edel too, even though she knew he had participated, but explaining him would have been a nuisance. Besides, she thought it was cooler this way. She'd also left out Rentt's use of divinity and fusion arts, but those were something of a secret weapon for him, so she replaced them with spirit for her story. As for the bittersweet conclusion, that was her own dramatic flair.

Lorraine looked at Riri and Fahri to gauge their reaction. They were still staring bright-eyed at the figure of the robed man before the fallen tarasque. It appeared she'd done an excellent job at maintaining Rentt's reputation with them. Lorraine was satisfied.

After wandering around the village for a while to help myself calm down, I returned home. There I encountered my two childhood friends. They were looking at me with immense respect, but I had no idea what I'd done to deserve that, especially considering this was the first time I'd seen them since I'd returned to the village.

"Rentt, you're so strong! I had no idea!" Riri said animatedly.

Fahri calmly added, "Ren, you took down that crazy thing like it was nothing. Adventurers are awesome."

They stared at me with big smiles. Their slightly red faces told me they were excited about something, but I couldn't figure out what. From the way they looked at me, I had my guesses as to what they were feeling, but I didn't know what caused it.

That was when I saw Lorraine sitting on a log behind them. She looked proud, but maybe that was my imagination. Although, I had gotten used to how Lorraine expressed herself over the last decade, and if I thought she felt a certain way, I was almost always right. But again I didn't know why.

From the look of things, Riri and Fahri must have visited the house while Lorraine was there, and they ended up talking. Their respect probably came from something Lorraine had said about my work in Maalt. I could imagine she had exaggerated to some extent. The "crazy thing" Fahri referred to was most likely a tarasque, a giant skeleton, or something of that nature. That said, it would have been hard to describe the power of those monsters to these girls who'd lived in a mountain village all their life. Plus, Lorraine tended to sound more explanatory than anything. She was easily understood, but she lacked emotion. It was like sitting through a lecture. It wouldn't have made my childhood friends act this way. That's when it hit me. Lorraine knew illusion magic.

Illusion magic was primarily used to project images of maps or structures in the air. These spells were known for being immensely challenging to construct, and they cost a lot of mana to sustain. Those who used this magic worked at theaters throughout the world and supplemented the mana cost with large amounts of magic crystals. Illusions were far more effective than simple painted backdrops, so they were often used in classy theaters. In Lorraine's case, though, she could project and sustain huge images on her own. By researching magic circles and their construction, she had even figured out how to substantially reduce the mana cost. At least, that was what I assumed. When I'd asked her before how she did it, she'd given me an incomprehensible answer. This knowledge would be worth a fortune, but I had been utterly unable to use the magic at the time, and it had all seemed too complicated for me. Maybe now I could understand it if I tried, but I would have to start from the basics.

In any case, if Lorraine used illusion magic to project an image of me fighting a monster, it would explain her satisfaction and their awe. That left the question of exactly how much she spiced it up. To be honest, my battles with the giant skeleton and the tarasque were pretty lame. The giant skeleton was the first giant monster I had ever fought on my own. I happened to beat it by hitting its weak point, but one incorrect move could have ended me. And I only beat the tarasque with Edel's help. Demidragon or not, nothing related to dragons was easy to defeat. If she depicted these fights accurately, I would have barely managed to win, but the sparkling eyes of my childhood friends told me that she had stretched the truth.

"Riri, Fahri, long time no see. Did Lorraine show you her illusion magic or something?"

"Yeah," Riri answered. "City people are pretty amazing. Those illusions looked so real. I never knew magic could do stuff like that! You looked so cool when you fought that monster, and the monster looked terrifying!"

"I guess this is what you can do when you master magic," Fahri added. "Looks like you've gotten really strong since moving to the city, Ren. Made me think I should go train in the city at some point myself."

My assumption seemed to be spot on. Still, I felt that their excitement was overblown. I hadn't gotten that much stronger, and the power I now possessed was a matter of luck. Whether that luck was good or bad, it was hard to say. Lorraine's illusion magic was also beyond the bounds of normalcy. Whether Riri and Fahri went to the city or not, they had virtually zero chance of becoming a magician on her level. The only reason Lorraine stopped at Silver-class was because she didn't take many jobs, but she could easily reach Gold-class. Besides that, she excelled more with non-combat-oriented magic. She was an adventurer and knew how to fight, but more than that, she was a researcher and scholar. Her talent for constructing theories was beyond what the average magician could hope to achieve. If Riri and Fahri thought this was normal in the city, they had another thing coming.

"Lorraine is pretty unique even among city folk," I said. "I wouldn't go to the city expecting everyone to be like her."

"Are you unique too, Rentt?" Riri asked. "That poison didn't even work on you."

"Well, uh, that's nothing special…" I wasn't expecting to hear that and didn't know how to respond.

"So there are a bunch of people that aren't affected by poison? They're that strong? I knew the city was something special," Fahri remarked.

At the very least, poison was perfectly effective against humans regardless of where they came from. My own circumstances were just a bit different. I wanted to shout this at them, but it would be hard to explain. This was a dreadful misunderstanding, and I would have to take my time clearing it up for the duration of our stay in the village. I didn't know how to convince my childhood friends that Maalt wasn't a city full of freakish superhumans, but I decided that would be one of my goals while we were here.

"By the way, Riri, didn't you want to ask Lorraine something?" Fahri said as if suddenly remembering something.

Riri stared at me and Lorraine. "I was just so distracted by our chat about Rentt and the city. Now I have to go prepare for tonight. Lorraine, can we talk again later?" Riri asked.

Lorraine cocked her head, but she saw no reason to object. "Sure, that should be fine. But tonight is that banquet the mayor and his wife mentioned, isn't it?"

"Yeah, there's that. Fahri and I are gonna help cook and stuff, so we actually don't have much time."

"I see. Sorry for keeping you."

"No, it was us who were keeping you. It was nice hearing your stories. See you later. You too, Rentt," Riri said and waved goodbye.

Fahri waved as well. "I'd love to see more illusions like that tonight. I think everyone would. Bye now, you two."

"What were they here for in the first place?" I asked.

"Who knows? They wanted to talk to you, I think," Lorraine answered, but she looked unsure.

"So, you used illusion magic to show them some things."

Lorraine gulped, but a moment later she proudly puffed out her chest. "Yes, indeed I did. I didn't want to reveal your secret, nor did I want to damage your reputation within the village, so I tweaked the story somewhat. It wasn't easy, but you saw how they were. I would consider that quite the success."

Now I understood what had compelled Lorraine to use illusion magic to tell a story. If Riri and Fahri had asked what I was like in Maalt, it was probably hard for Lorraine to turn them down, and it was easier to show than to tell. Lorraine could be surprisingly willing to accommodate, and she had no reservations about using magic, unlike the majority of magicians. They withheld their magic in an effort to raise its value. Most magicians also didn't have much mana to spare, so they couldn't cast magic freely, but Lorraine had so much mana it was barely an issue.

"Well, it was nice of you to go through the effort, but Riri and Fahri were looking at me like I was some great hero. Maybe you overdid it a little."

"You think so?" Lorraine asked, a bit perturbed. "I do actually think you've done incredible things, so it wouldn't have been much different if I simply told the story verbally. Few adventurers even come across giant skeletons or tarasques, and defeating them solo is a feat worthy of praise."

She could be right about that, but any Gold-class adventurer could slay a tarasque. Giant skeletons were even weaker, simple enough for Silver-class adventurers to vanquish handily, if not even lower classes. It was nothing to boast about, so I told her as much.

Lorraine sighed. "You think too little of yourself. Consider how powerful you've become already. You left this village when you were young and came to Maalt with aspirations of becoming an adventurer. How much of what you can do now were you able to do back then? Your accomplishments could very well make you a hero in the eyes of this village."

When she put it that way, maybe she was right. It wasn't too long ago that I was the sort of Bronze-class adventurer you could find anywhere. For adventurers who came from villages of this size, that was the limit, at which point they would retire from adventuring and return to the village to become a hunter or guard of some sort. There was a good chance that would have happened to me at some point. It hadn't, but only thanks to my good luck, which may have also been bad luck. Now I could even fight tarasques, so from the perspective of all those downtrodden adventurers, I had achieved plenty.

After everything that had happened lately, I was starting to lose my confidence. I kept encountering enigmatic people like Laura and Nive, and it made me feel like I was nobody special. It was as if they were born with this aura of individuality, something that made them special, and I didn't know how to get that for myself.

Although, Laura notwithstanding, I didn't want to be like Nive. She was unique, to be sure, but to an inhuman extreme.

The way she thought and behaved had no place in society. Despite that, she had plenty of connections, and she had influence within a religious organization, so she navigated society strangely well. Regardless, she was a special case, and I didn't intend to follow her lead.

"I'll try to be a bit more confident. Anyway, Lorraine, show me the same illusion you showed them. I want to know exactly what it was in case they ask about it later."

"Good idea," Lorraine agreed. "I could explain by mouth, but it'll probably be quicker and easier to watch for yourself. Come with me."

Lorraine started to use her magic. It always looked complicated to me, but she found it so simple that she could hum while she did it. Once the spell was complete, Lorraine began to control it.

All I could do was ask who this man was supposed to be. Lorraine had embellished the story to a ludicrous degree, and Edel wasn't even there. I also made it out virtually unharmed in her version. It was true I hadn't suffered any serious injuries, but I'd gone through a lot to reach the tarasque and had gotten fairly beaten up in the process. This made it look like I dispatched the tarasque effortlessly. Now Riri and Fahri's stares made perfect sense.

"I'm sure you realize this, but this is pretty excessive," I complained.

"I could have presented you like a legendary king, so I'd say I restrained myself. Don't worry about it," she said, disregarding my concerns.

Every country had legends about the king or queen who founded the nation, and they were always highly exaggerated. Presenting a Bronze-class adventurer in the same light would be absurd, but when I looked at Lorraine's face, I could tell she was half-serious.

"Lorraine."

"What?"

"Are you planning to show this again at the banquet tonight?"

"Of course. They asked me to," Lorraine said with amusement.

I was already weary, but now I had to spend the rest of the day thinking about how to show the villagers tonight at the banquet what I was actually like. I never came up with an answer.

Chapter 2: A Welcome Banquet and Rentt's Origins

At the center of the village, fire blazed in the town square. The tops of the wooden watchtowers were lit up, illuminating the darkness of night. Around the towers, tables covered with food cooked by the village women lined the outdoor area.

Among the dishes were those that included roasted birds and beasts caught by the hunters, crude meals typical of a small village. Such cooking was seldom seen in Maalt. Not that Maalt was that urban—these types of dishes could be found there—but a real metropolis like the capital would never serve anything so simple. It had no class, they would say. An especially rare catch would be different, but it still wasn't something they would eat on a daily basis. This village didn't just eat hunted animals for feasts; they consumed them regularly. It was part of the village experience.

The villagers were eating and chatting among themselves. I was the guest of honor, so many of them walked over to express their joy over my return. Many asked about the city. The young girls were curious about the latest trends, while the men wanted to know how beautiful the women were. It was pretty predictable.

I'd bought trendy souvenirs in Maalt for the girls, so I took this time to hand them out. They had cost a pretty penny, but it wasn't a waste. It made my return trips to the village more comfortable. Of course, I had gifts for the older women as well.

I didn't give much of anything to the men, but they thought nothing of it. I told them about some unchaste shops in the city and offered to show them around when they'd saved up enough money to visit. That always delighted them. They were simple folks, thankfully.

I never frequented those establishments myself, by the way. That's not to say I wasn't interested, but I thought training was more important. Plus, you didn't want to go to those places when you were exhausted. Of course, now that I was undead, it was out of the question.

Lorraine came by while I was in the middle of this conversation with some young men. "Having fun?" she asked.

They all turned red when they saw her. They stared for a while until they remembered what they'd been talking about, at which point they looked extremely uncomfortable. "Rentt, I think I'm gonna go talk to those guys over there. See ya," one of them said. Then they all scattered like ants.

Lorraine watched them flee and cocked her head. "Did I do something wrong?"

"No, but we were discussing something not meant for women's ears," I said with a smile.

"I get it. Though, I wouldn't especially mind it. How innocent are these boys?"

Lorraine was an adventurer, and most adventurers were vulgar men. She could hear discussions like this at any guild or bar. A woman wouldn't be attacked if she intruded on one of these conversations, but she might be called some problematic things. However, Lorraine had been an adventurer so long she had grown used to it. In fact, she had learned to fire back at them with even more vile language, so much so that she left newer adventurers speechless. It was terrifying. Certainly nothing I would ever say to someone.

I never understood what was supposed to be fun about it, and when I overheard insults being thrown around, I assumed these people had nothing better to do. Not that I couldn't be dragged into some filthy conversations when no women were around. But that was only because it was socially appropriate in those circumstances.

"I guess the village men are pretty innocent," I said. "Try not to mess with them too much. If you convince them all to go to the city, the village will lose half its population."

"What do you mean by that?" she asked.

I wanted to tell her that the men who blushed and ran off had done so because of Lorraine's beauty, but she didn't seem to follow. I could have been direct and said they thought she was hot; they might think they could go out with plenty of beautiful women like her if they went to the city. I didn't know how to get that across without annoying her, though.

"Well, never mind that, then," I said and dropped the subject. Lorraine knew how to make crass jokes with men, but she was still oblivious when it counted the most.

"Hey, now I'm curious. Explain," she insisted.

"That might be a bit difficult. If you must know, go ask Riri or Fahri. I'm sure they'll know what I'm talking about. Oh, sounds like Jal and Dol are calling. I'll be back," I said and got myself out of there. I heard her shout at me from behind, but I pretended not to hear anything. It was the best solution I could come up with.

"Yeesh, what's with him?" Lorraine muttered. She was curious about what he meant, but there was no use thinking about it. That didn't stop her from trying to figure it out, though. She thought for a bit but couldn't come up with anything.

"Oh, Lorraine, what's wrong?" Riri asked. Fahri was with her, and they were both holding wooden cups.

The drinks in the wooden cups only had enough alcohol for preservation purposes and could hardly be considered alcoholic drinks, but they were nice and sweet. This was Hathara's specialty beverage. The men chose severely alcoholic drinks for themselves, but all the girls around Riri and Fahri's age drank this.

Lorraine, however, chose the strong alcohol for herself. Even that didn't seem to affect her. She calmly asked Riri and Fahri about what Rentt had meant a moment ago.

They appeared to immediately understand. "It's because you're beautiful, Lorraine. If a bunch of men go to the city thinking they'll find women like you, it'd be a problem for the village," Riri explained.

"Hm, am I beautiful?" Lorraine asked.

"Don't go around asking women that if you don't want to get smacked," Riri said with a scary smile. It sent chills down Lorraine's spine.

"Sorry. But I never knew Rentt saw me that way," she said.

If Riri's explanation was correct, then Rentt must have viewed her as beautiful. She hadn't thought he paid attention to her appearance, so this came as a shock. In that case, maybe there could be something more between them. Lorraine was a bit disappointed there wasn't.

Fahri decided to offer her opinion. "Ren's a little weird about these things. He can look at you in an objective sense and see that you're beautiful, but I don't think he knows what to do with those feelings."

Lorraine looked bitter. "How'd he end up like this?" she questioned half-jokingly.

Fahri's input seemed to strike the nail on the head. She had perfectly described Rentt's personality. He could look at a woman and say if he found her cute or pretty, but he had no idea what the next step should be. He'd been like that for as long as Lorraine had known him. Never in their ten years together had he said anything flirtatious. He wasn't a monk, and he had no reason to live a life of celibacy. She was the same in that regard, but she felt there might be another explanation.

That was what had prompted Lorraine to ask. But for some reason, Riri and Fahri reacted gravely to her question. She noticed how their expressions grew darker. She suspected that she had touched on a bad topic. It was too late to take it back though, so she tried to casually change the subject. It was the only way she could think of to make them feel better.

But before Lorraine could do so, Fahri spoke up. "Something happened with Ren a long time ago. I don't think he's ever been able to get over it."

Lorraine wondered what she meant but thought it rude to ask.

"Right, but it's not like anyone can change what happened," Riri said. "He really ought to forget about it. Or at least move on with his life."

It sounded like there was some tragedy in Rentt's past, but Lorraine still didn't think it was her place to ask.

"Lorraine, Ren was—" Fahri started, but Lorraine stopped her.

"As much as I'd like to hear about this, I don't think it would be right to discuss it while Rentt's not present. Let's hold off for now," she said.

"I see. Yes, you're right. I'm sorry, I shouldn't have brought it up," Fahri replied and apologetically bowed her head.

"It's fine," Lorraine said and vaguely shook her head.

Lorraine didn't blame them for mentioning it. They were worried about Rentt, so they wanted to tell her something that might help. She understood that. Whatever had happened left a deep scar in Rentt's heart. Knowing that Lorraine was friends with him for so long, they presumably wanted to convince her to offer him some support. There was nothing wrong with that. In fact, it was normal to do so when worried for someone. But if Lorraine was going to hear about Rentt's past, she wanted to hear it from the man himself.

Realistically, as long as she wasn't planning to go telling everyone, there was no issue hearing it from Riri and Fahri. Rentt was unlikely to have a problem with it either. But Lorraine was an adventurer, and you never looked into another adventurer's history. It wasn't an official rule, but it became common sense. Adventurers often had unpleasant secrets. Uncovering their pasts could unearth some dreadful things. The rule was based on that unfortunate reality, but now it was an act of kindness between adventurers. If Lorraine asked anyone but Rentt about a formative event in his past, she would never live it down. But this was something only adventurers understood, so communicating that to Riri and Fahri would be difficult. That was why she hadn't been more specific when she'd asked Fahri to wait. Still, she felt bad about that.

"I know you're worried about Rentt and want to help, so don't worry about it. Besides, I think I'll ask him about it myself later. If he doesn't want to talk about it, then that's all right. If he doesn't mind, then we'll discuss it like any ordinary topic. That's always how it's been with him," Lorraine said in a way she thought was nonchalant.

Riri and Fahri thought Lorraine looked a bit excited. "You're awfully close, aren't you?" Riri asked.

"I can see you have an unbreakable bond," Fahri said.

For a moment, Lorraine wondered what they were talking about, but after a bit of thought, she found that they were correct. "We are close, yes, and I suppose we have something of a bond," she said.

Lorraine had meant nothing more than that they were connected as fellow adventurers or friends, but Riri and Fahri seemed strangely disappointed to hear it.

"Oh right, I was planning on showing off that illusion magic to everyone, if that's all right. If it would scare the children and the elderly, then maybe I shouldn't."

"I'd love to see it again," Riri said. "I don't think anyone would be upset by something so silly. Go right ahead."

"Wait a second, Riri!" Fahri cried. "They'll think we're under attack by a monster! We at least have to tell the mayor to inform everyone first!"

Fahri was likely correct in this instance. A tarasque would never show up in these mountains, but giant skeletons weren't impossible. They needed to inform the villagers that illusion magic was about to be used and that it didn't pose any threat. Riri claimed it would be fine, but it still could be a bit much for children and the elderly. It might be best to point out that she could make sure some people couldn't see it, in case of any fears it could cause heart problems or panic attacks. Lorraine informed them of this, and Riri and Fahri nodded and ran to Rentt's foster father.

Lorraine thought she should go with them, but they had looked at the cup in her hand and insisted that she stay where she was.

They must have assumed she was drunk. The type of drink was easily distinguished by the shape of the cup, so it was clear that Lorraine had taken the stronger alcohol. Most of the villagers with this drink were stumbling around and looking like they could trip into a bonfire at any moment, so maybe their decision was only natural. In reality, the drink had little effect on her. Lorraine held her liquor remarkably well and seldom got drunk. Sometimes she acted drunk, but only to fit in with a drunken crowd, and even then her mind was sharp.

"We informed the mayor! He says he's going to tell everyone," Riri and Fahri said as they returned. The mayor made his announcement soon afterward. He did an effective job relaying Lorraine's warnings and declared that the event would take place where he was standing. Now Lorraine wished she had gone with Riri and Fahri to save time.

As she began to walk to the location, Riri and Fahri attended her.

"What is it? I appreciate having two pretty ladies all over me, but why?" Lorraine joked.

"Well, we're worried you might be drunk," Riri said awkwardly.

"I'm not the least bit drunk. I'm sure that means nothing coming from someone you believe to be drunk, but look, I can walk in a straight line," Lorraine declared and demonstrated for them.

They seemed surprised. "Even the largest adults can't walk right after having a glass of Hathara's strongest alcohol. I've never seen someone keep it together so well," Fahri said.

"Really? This is my fourth cup," Lorraine replied.

Riri muttered, "Are you some kind of freak?"

But Lorraine finally convinced them she was fine, so they let her walk to the mayor on her own.

"Maybe I really am a bit drunk," Lorraine murmured to herself. She had presented Rentt's battles with the giant skeleton and the tarasque again, but it was at least thirty percent flashier than her presentation to Riri and Fahri. The people of Hathara didn't seem to have a problem with that; rather, they quite liked it. Many said they never thought Rentt was such a successful adventurer. Some said they would even propose to him if he still lived in the village. Maybe she had overdone it, but it was too late to undo it now.

Lorraine feared that Rentt might complain, but when she looked around, he was nowhere to be seen. She had thought he would want to witness her illusion magic with his own eyes, but that didn't seem to be the case. Maybe he'd had enough of being treated like a hero. Particularly after this extravagant display, he might have ditched as soon as it ended so the villagers wouldn't fawn over him.

Lorraine looked around for anyone who might have seen Rentt. She spotted Riri and approached her. Riri saw Lorraine coming and complimented her on this latest portrayal of Rentt's feats. After listening to the praise for a while, Lorraine shifted to the topic at hand. "By the way, Riri, do you know where Rentt is? I'm guessing he watched the show, but I don't see him anywhere. I want to ask for his opinion."

"Rentt's not here? Hm, I could swear I saw him a moment ago. Maybe he ran off," Riri pondered, coming to the same conclusion as Lorraine. "Well, he must be somewhere. Just keep searching. If I happen to see him, I'll mention that you're looking for him."

"Thanks, please do," Lorraine said and walked away.

Riri now seemed much more receptive to Lorraine, as if they were close friends. Lorraine guessed that the people of Rentt's village were quick to bond with others, much like Rentt himself.

Lorraine spent a while searching for Rentt, but he wasn't anywhere near the watchtowers.

"Lorraine, are you having fun?" Ingo asked.

"Yes, very much so. All the villagers are so nice and cheerful, and the food is delicious. I've also taken quite a liking to this," Lorraine said and held up her cup.

"There aren't a lot of women who can handle those drinks," Ingo pointed out, his eyes wide. "But I'm glad you're enjoying yourself. There isn't much to do here in Hathara, so I was worried a city person would find it hard to fit in."

"Oh, it's not so bad. In fact, there's plenty here that you would never find in Maalt. It's been an interesting experience." Food and drink aside, Lorraine didn't know of many villages like this one. As a scholar and an adventurer, Hathara piqued her curiosity.

"Is that right? I don't think it's an especially interesting place, but I've lived here so long that maybe I wouldn't know. By the way…"

"Yes? What is it?"

"It looked like you were looking for something. What do you need?" Ingo asked.

Now Lorraine knew why he'd gone out of his way to talk to her. Lorraine was wandering around on her own, so he'd assumed she had some sort of problem. She appreciated his thoughtfulness.

"Yes, I was looking for Rentt. I haven't seen him anywhere. Do you know where he went?" Lorraine asked.

"Rentt? You're right, he doesn't seem to be around. I wonder where he could be," Ingo said and thought to himself.

"You don't have to find him for me. If you don't know, then that's fine."

"I have a guess as to where he could be, though. He's probably somewhere over there, if you'd like to go check. We don't want the guest of honor away from the banquet for too long."

Ingo pointed to the other end of the village. It was dark and difficult to traverse at this time of night, but only for ordinary people. Lorraine was an experienced magician and adventurer, so this posed no problem for her. She had many means of dealing with darkness, but this time she chose the simplest. She conjured up an orb of light. Ingo was a bit surprised to see it, but he knew that Lorraine was a magician, so he was quick to calm down again. That kind of courage was hard to come by in a small-town mayor.

"I'll go take a look, then. Thanks for telling me," Lorraine said and walked off to where she was directed.

Some time later, she stopped at a large building. It was possibly the largest structure in the village, albeit nothing compared to what Maalt and even larger cities had to offer. Judging by the decor, it appeared to be a church.

"I don't know what religion this is for, but I suppose even villages in the mountains still need places of worship," Lorraine murmured. This church didn't belong to the Church of the Eastern Sky, the Lobelians, or any other major religion, but that was typical of small villages. If they had local gods or spirits, they would turn any given building into a church as long as it was big enough.

But Rentt was nowhere to be seen. If he had gone anywhere, Lorraine thought it was probably here, but maybe she was off the mark. Or so she thought, but then she sensed someone behind the church. It seemed that she was right after all.

When Lorraine went around to the back of the church, Rentt was there, sitting on the ground. Lorraine looked at him and wondered what she should do, but there was no way he didn't sense her at this distance. She extinguished her orb of light and boldly approached.

She sat down next to Rentt. "Is this a graveyard?" Lorraine asked without looking at him.

Rentt was staring at a gravestone. "Yes, my parents are buried here. I figured I should give them a visit."

"Sorry I got in the way," Lorraine promptly replied. When reflecting on those who had passed, the presence of others could be a nuisance. Rentt was meeting with the dead, and Lorraine didn't want to bother him. Nobody should interrupt that.

"No, it's fine," Rentt said. He grabbed her arm as she tried to leave. "I'm guessing Papa told you I was here."

He must have meant Ingo, but earlier Rentt had called him "Dad." Lorraine wondered if he consciously referred to him as "Papa" now because he was at his parents' graves. If it was an unconscious choice, she thought it best not to dig too deep.

"How did you know? You didn't think I'd find this place myself?"

"We're pretty far removed from the rest of the village, and you know I've been hard to detect ever since I became undead. Even you couldn't have found me on your own this easily. Besides, Papa knows I always come here when I visit home. This place makes me lose track of the time. I stay so long someone inevitably has to come get me."

Maybe that was why Ingo hadn't mentioned this was a graveyard. If he had, Lorraine might have refrained from coming. But if what Rentt said was true, searching for him here was a common occurrence, so she had no reason to feel bad. Lorraine decided she might as well stay and took a seat.

"Besides, as long as you're in town, you should visit my parents with me," Rentt continued. "You're the best friend I have outside the village. I'm sure my parents would love to meet you."

"I see. Then don't mind if I do," Lorraine said. She kneeled before the gravestones and held her hands together in prayer. "Hello, Rentt's parents. My name is Lorraine Vivie. I've been friends with your son for ten years." She introduced herself and then talked about their memories together in Maalt. "Rentt and I will be seeing plenty more of each other in the future too. I pray you watch over us from the heavens," she said in conclusion.

"It really hit me just now how much we've been through together," Rentt muttered. He'd experienced those events himself and had those memories too, but hearing about them from another perspective sounded strange.

"You do have a tendency to get yourself in trouble. Compared to your plethora of recent problems, though, your old issues were the sort every adventurer deals with."

"True. I never thought I'd visit the graves of the dead while being dead myself. I was kind of looking forward to that."

"Why? How would it have been any different from before?"

"I thought maybe I'd have the ability to see spirits now and could see my parents. But I was let down, unfortunately."

"Spirits? That would be difficult. It's said that most souls pass through the Gate of the Dead without lingering in this world. There's no way to summon them back, short of being a necromancer. But even in those cases, it's unclear as to whether they're truly spirits."

"Well, yeah, I know that. I wasn't that serious. It's fine," Rentt claimed, but he looked a bit disappointed. He may have had higher expectations than he wanted to admit.

"Sorry to bring this up, but weren't your parents killed by monsters?" Lorraine asked, feeling it would be strange not to touch on the subject while they sat at their graves. He didn't have to discuss it if he didn't want to. If he didn't, Lorraine was confident he would change the subject.

"Yeah, they were," Rentt said, less gravely than Lorraine expected. "They'd gone to a nearby village to sell our village's special products. They were unlucky, to be honest. Normally they would've sold the goods to a traveling merchant who'd take them to the village himself, but he happened to be late. Winter was approaching, and we were in desperate need of money to buy necessities. That was why my parents and I, along with the mayor's mother and daughter, went to the nearby village."

"The names of my parents are carved on their graves. My father was Locusta, and my mother was Melissa. Locusta had rugged looks and a strong build. I never thought we looked much alike, but my foster parents still say I have his eyes. As for my stature, I inherited more from my mother, but she was beautiful and popular. My parents had already been married a while, but men still jokingly proposed to her. She turned them all down, of course.

"Oh right, and there was the mayor's mother, my foster grandmother. Her name was Pravda. She resembled the medicine woman I've mentioned before. They were sisters, so maybe that should be obvious. The medicine woman would look just like her if her face was a bit more slender and a lot less wicked. But I guess that doesn't tell you anything. I didn't see her anywhere at the banquet, but if we go to see her tomorrow, you'll know what I'm talking about. Everyone's first impression of Gharb is that she's a cruel old lady, and if you spend some time with her, you'll learn you were right to think so. Most of the village kids are afraid of her. She can be surprisingly kind on occasion, but enough about her for now.

"We only brought such an old woman along because Pravda was to act as a representative of the mayor's family. The mayor's daughter came to watch her grandmother do her job. And she came because I was going too. We were close friends. Well, you could say we were sort of betrothed. My parents grew up with her parents.

They were friends their whole lives, and they all wanted us to get married. I could have said no, but I was five years old at the time and didn't think much of it. I did like her, though. Maybe I would've considered it when we got older, but instead, I can only wonder what might have been.

"Anyway, that was our group. I thought for sure this would be a fun journey. Our destination was the closest village to ours, so given the distance, I don't know if journey is even the right word for it. Regardless, none of Hathara's horses had much stamina for drawing carriages, so the trip was going to take two or three days. As for the end result of that journey, I think you can already guess."

"Rentt, Jinlin, are you finished packing?" my mother asked me and the mayor's daughter. Moving the luggage into the carriage was a job for my father and the young men of the village, so Jinlin and I didn't have much to do.

"Yeah, we're done," I said.

"All finished! I'm ready to go any time!" Jinlin answered after me.

"All right, then get in the carriage. Just about all the luggage should be loaded by now," my mother said with a smile.

Jinlin and I headed that way. She chattered as we walked. "Hey, Rentt, what do you think the other village is like? I've never been to another village before. I can't wait!"

I'd never been outside the village either, and neither had most of the village children under the age of ten. There could be monsters or thieves out there. Not that many thieves bothered to come anywhere near a remote village like Hathara, but some stray exiles made their living in the area. Monsters, on the other hand, attacked anyone regardless of the profit potential. Adults could flee from average monsters, but it was best for children to stay home.

There were exceptions, however. If a child was expected to be a village leader in the future, their parents or other relatives would bring them outside the village while they were still young. Jinlin was one such case.

My parents weren't leaders of anything, and my father wasn't from the village. He traveled for a long time before settling down in Hathara, and the villagers valued his experience. He was often picked to represent the village when it was necessary to travel outside it. And my mother wanted to come with him, so they couldn't very well leave me behind (unless they left me with someone, as they had done before). But I was five now, and they thought it was time for me to get used to traveling. They hoped I would one day take my father's place for these excursions.

At the time, though, I was still a small child and couldn't tell Jinlin anything. "I don't know," I said. "But it has to be scary out there. I hope we don't see any monsters."

"You're such a scaredy-cat, Rentt. Just say you'll beat up all the monsters!" Jinlin shouted. She was a rough and rowdy type, the sort who loved to climb trees and play with toy swords. By contrast, I was an introvert and preferred to quietly play with building blocks at home.

"That's a surprise," Lorraine said. "Knowing you, I thought you would've been waving around a wooden sword even back then."

"Not at all," I replied with a bitter laugh. "Well, you're not that far off. I started training soon after this. Anyway, that was the kid I was back then."

"A sweet, shy one?"

"I also looked pretty feminine, but not because I was trying to. To some extent I still do, but everyone said I looked like a girl when I grew my hair out. I was also timid, and I was never one to go climb trees myself."

The way I remembered it, I had a womanly personality. I didn't know if that had actually changed much since then, but I couldn't imagine anyone looking at me at the time and guessing I'd become an adventurer.

"That's quite a shock. Well, your face may have looked feminine. But years of adventuring will harden a man, so I suppose that changed things," Lorraine said.

"So my face has the air of an adventurer, you say?" I asked jokingly.

"It's hard to tell right now, considering the mask," she replied.

"That's too bad. Well, let me get on with the story."

"Oh, you'll beat the monsters for us, Jinlin?" Pravda asked while Jinlin and I were talking.

"Yeah!" Jinlin shouted. "I was playing adventurer with Jal and Dol the other day. They were the goblins, and I was the adventurer. I totally slayed them."

"Is this true, Rentt?" Pravda asked me.

"Yeah. I was the receptionist at the guild," I answered.

Pravda cocked her head. "I think you have your roles reversed," she muttered.

Now that I thought about it, she was right. We played out the roles we wanted to, though, so nobody could complain—except Jal and Dol, who did nothing but complain. They always lost at rock-paper-scissors and didn't get a choice. They were extremely predictable, so Jinlin always won. She was an oddly smart girl. As for me, I just did what Jinlin said, so I always won too. We were kind of conspiring against them, but it was fun.

"Jinlin, monsters might be easy to beat when you play pretend, but real ones are fearsome," Pravda lectured. "If we're attacked on this journey, promise me you'll run away."

Pravda always had a kind, peaceful demeanor, but on this one occasion, she sounded harsh. Considering the topic at hand, it made sense.

Jinlin wasn't often obedient, but she seemed to listen this time. "I know, I heard the same thing yesterday. I'll be fine!" she insisted.

"Rentt, I'd say the same to you, but I'm sure you'll run away on your own."

"Of course. Nothing's more important than your life."

"Good. For a boy, though, you're not very ambitious. Jinlin, what is it you like about him?"

"I like that he's brave," Jinlin answered. It was hard to see any bravery in me at the time, so Pravda was confused by her answer.

A while later, she stared at me. "I don't see it," she said. "There *is* something interesting about him, but bravery? Well, if you say so. Now, it's about time to depart. Let's get on the carriage."

From the moment we departed that morning, the carriage moved nonstop until we reached our destination. Jinlin, looking green in the face and rather ill from motion sickness, asked me if we had arrived. Despite all her braggadocio earlier, she had the most unexpected vulnerabilities. I had also never been on a carriage before, but I handled the long trip perfectly fine. Even now, I can read books on a carriage ride and not get sick. Our personalities suggested we'd have the opposite reactions, but the human body is hard to comprehend.

"Yeah, we're here, Jinlin. Are you all right? You can throw up if you need to," I said.

"I'm just fine," Jinlin claimed while holding her mouth, "but I hope we can go outside and get some fresh air. Can we, Grandma?"

"My goodness, you're just like your father when he was young," Pravda remarked. "Fine, go outside. But we're about to unload the luggage, so don't go too far."

Under normal circumstances, Jinlin would have explored around, but she was in no state to do that. We left the carriage and found ourselves at a loading dock for some company. It was so late that no other carriages were around. This was a small town, so few people would sell their cargo here regardless. The loading dock was small and mostly for merchants to load their wares.

Thankfully, Hathara's products went for a high price in any town. My father, thanks to his travels, also knew the value of goods throughout the region, so we could sell for an appropriate price wherever we went. If not, we would have made more traveling all the way to a city like Maalt, even considering the cost of transit. But that would also increase the chances of encountering thieves or monsters, so it had its advantages and disadvantages. Hathara wasn't big enough to need that much money or resources anyway, to be honest.

"Ugh, I feel awful," Jinlin said even after we were outside.

The loading dock was under a roof and didn't feel very open, so I thought a more spacious area would make her feel better. "Jinlin, this way," I said and dragged her with me. Not that far, of course, because I remembered what Pravda had said. We could still see the carriage, at least.

Now that we were in a more open location, Jinlin finally seemed to calm down. She took a few deep breaths and got over her motion sickness. "I think I'll be okay now," she said.

"That's good. Should we go back?"

Jinlin looked dissatisfied. "We came all this way, though! I want to see the town! Let's go, Rentt," she said and dragged me around by the arm.

"No! Pravda said not to go too far away."

"We don't have to listen to that old lady. She's always telling me what to do. Nothing wrong with making her worry sometimes," Jinlin argued. Of course, I doubted she was serious. She looked more uneasy than angry, more pouty than hateful.

Jinlin was the only daughter of the mayor, so she would one day be forced to lead the village. Looking back on it now, her upbringing must have been rough. Even at the age of five, she had a number of skills. She could read and write at an elementary level, and she knew all about the village's special products, how they were made, and which families produced what. That could only come from a strict education. I would bet that she was often jealous when she saw kids her age running around having fun while she had to study. That would explain why she was so rebellious when she did get to have some fun.

I was still young and didn't think much about it at the time, but I had some idea about the conflicts in Jinlin's life, so I found it hard to tell her no in earnest. I ended up accompanying Jinlin around the village. In hindsight, I should have stood my ground.

"You certainly are different now, but it sounds like you always had a tendency to get dragged into trouble," Lorraine said.

I agreed with her. "I never made my own decisions back then. I was passive and submissive, while Jinlin was the opposite, so that was how things often went. Nowadays it's me getting myself in trouble, if anything."

My encounters with the dragon and with Nive Maris might never have happened if not for my strange curiosity. Considering my bad luck, though, maybe I would've just ended up in some other crisis.

"Well, any adventurer is going to run into danger sometimes. That's the nature of the job," Lorraine said, trying to console me.

It was true that danger came with being an adventurer. If you didn't like it, then you picked the wrong profession. Surviving required some caution, and I thought I was cautious enough. If I died regardless, then I couldn't necessarily complain. Adventurers lived on the edge. That was why they were treated as ruffians.

"But, well, it's not like I was an adventurer at the time. I should have stopped Jinlin."

The town was a spectacle to behold. Of course, it wasn't even as big as Maalt, to say nothing of other cities. But to me back then, it was like I'd arrived in the big city. The stores carried all sorts of things my village lacked, the people dressed better than anyone back home, and the buildings towered higher than anything I had ever seen.

Jinlin and I chatted about those buildings, wondering if nobles lived there and if the castles of kings were even larger. It was fun, and it reminded me of how small and irrelevant Hathara was. But it didn't make me hate my hometown so much as it taught me about what else the world had to offer.

I don't know how Jinlin felt, but she probably thought similarly. Looking back on it now, I'm glad I could see the good sides of both Hathara and the city. Plenty of villages were destitute and difficult to survive in, but Hathara was livable enough despite its location. We were too excited to think about that at the moment, though.

We were just beginning to tire from walking around when Jinlin asked, "Rentt, do you hear a voice?"

"No, I don't hear anything," I answered. But a moment later, I heard a voice screaming for help. It was so oddly shrill it sounded inhuman.

Surprised, I looked around to find the source. Jinlin did the same, but we didn't find anything.

"Maybe someone's playing a trick," I suggested.

Jinlin shook her head. "No way! I know what I'm hearing!"

The voice was actually loud and clear, and even if this were some sort of joke, the sound had to be coming from somewhere. We searched everywhere, and after a while, the voice got fed up and told us to look up. I hadn't even realized we hadn't done so, but humans seldom pay attention to what's above them.

We did what the voice said and saw a long branch. A little person's clothes were caught on the tip, and they were dangling in the air. By little, I don't mean they were a child. They were barely fifteen centimeters tall, almost like a toy.

I was shocked, but Jinlin wasn't. She knew what she was seeing. "Rentt! That's a fairy! Mother says they almost never show themselves around humans!" she exclaimed feverishly.

I wasn't so exhilarated. "Shouldn't we help it? It looks like it can't get off."

"Don't you get excited about anything? If I'd encountered a fairy when I was five, I would have been as jubilant as Jinlin. Like a normal child," Lorraine stated.

"Well, I was at least a little bit excited, but the fairy looked like it was in agony. I mean, it was screaming all that time, so I think I was being sensible," I said. It wasn't an excuse; it was the truth.

"Well, when you put it that way, I understand how you felt somewhat."

"Right? Let's move on."

"Oh, right. We have to help it! But how?" Jinlin said.

Thankfully, Jinlin and I were children, so we were sincere in our desire to help. But the fairy was caught on the branch of a tall tree. We weren't tall enough to reach it, and even an adult would have found it difficult. Still, someone taller would have a better chance, so I made a suggestion.

"Let's tell an adult," I said. "Maybe they could reach." That seemed like the best method.

Jinlin agreed, so we tried asking some strangers in the area. In retrospect, that was a pretty dangerous move, but the town seemed friendly enough. We weren't kidnapped, at least. But there was a problem. We tried to explain that there was a fairy dangling from a branch, but nobody understood. They looked at the branch but acted like they didn't see anything.

Now I know there are many types of fairies, some of which are visible to everyone, and some of which can only be seen by humans with mana. Neither of us knew that back then, though, so it made us feel like liars. We were certain it was true, but nobody believed us.

It was sad for sure, but we refused to give up. The fairy was starting to tire out, so we had to save it fast.

Jinlin saw the urgency before I did. "Rentt, I'll climb up and save it!" she said.

"Jinlin, that's dangerous! Stop!" I shouted from below as she climbed the tree, but she didn't listen.

I wished she wasn't so gung-ho about things, but she was great at climbing trees in Hathara, surprisingly so for a five-year-old. However, she always climbed the same kind; she wasn't used to this one. The trees in our village were short, and the ground beneath them was made up of dirt and grass, so falling wouldn't lead to a substantial injury. The adults allowed it as long as they were present to make sure nothing happened. This tree, however, was completely different. It was extremely tall, and the ground below was hard so that carriages could cross over it. If a child were to fall, they could easily be injured.

Regardless, she kept climbing.

I should have called an adult. Since a child was now climbing a tall tree, it would have been easier to convince them to help. But I was a child too, so the idea didn't occur to me. I just knew she was in danger and I had to get her to come down, so I kept shouting from the bottom of the tree.

But Jinlin was too stubborn to listen. Maybe she was so focused on climbing and saving the fairy that she didn't hear me. I was worried to death, but Jinlin's climbing skills were hard to deny. After a few attempts, she got the hang of this new kind of tree. She pulled herself up there like a monkey, and soon enough, she reached the branch where the fairy was stuck. After that, of course, she was going to climb along the branch to get to the tip. Honestly, the branch wasn't that thin. It looked strong enough to hold a child—but no more than that. Climbing on it was definitely dangerous, but Jinlin did so without issue.

The crackling of the branch sounded wretched to my ears. I thought it would snap at any moment. As Jinlin approached the tip, it bent further and further. But she still kept going.

Jinlin reached her hand out to the fairy. "Here, I'll help you," she whispered. She didn't look at all afraid of falling, and in fact she seemed excited in a way. Helping this fairy was electrifying to her.

The fairy saw her hand but appeared to be a bit intimidated. It was probably scared to be crushed. If you were the size of a fairy, a human child would be like a giant to you. Jinlin seemed to realize this and changed her plan, progressing further along the branch. She slowly pulled the fairy free, but just then...

The branch snapped.

"Jinlin!" I cried and ran to the spot just below her. I had no time to think, and it never occurred to me that this was dangerous and that I should get out of the way. I just knew that Jinlin was in trouble and I had to do something.

As Jinlin was about to fall, she grasped the fairy tight and held it close to her chest. She was likely trying to protect it. Fairies could usually fly, but this one didn't have the energy to do so.

Just before Jinlin hit the ground, I got right below her. But I was young and couldn't catch her that elegantly. I was at least able to soften the impact of the fall, though. She fell heavily on my hands and chest. Unable to hold her steady, I collapsed. The sound of the branch hitting the ground was surprisingly quiet, but it was light enough to snap under a child's weight, so maybe that was to be expected.

Jinlin groaned in anguish as she lay on top of me.

"Jinlin, are you all right?" I asked, pain rushing through my whole body.

"Yeah, it doesn't hurt that much," she answered.

When I actually looked at her, she didn't seem to have any serious wounds. That was when I knew I'd made the right decision. Next, I looked at myself. I wasn't especially injured either. I had some scrapes and bruises, but nothing worse than what I'd gotten before from running around the village.

"Never do anything that dangerous ever again," I said. Maybe I should have yelled at her, but I wasn't capable of that at the time. This was the only way I could express myself. I must have looked pretty sad. I was pretty enraged on the inside, but I wasn't one to show my anger.

"Yeah, okay. I'm sorry," Jinlin replied.

"Jinlin, you're actually listening?" I asked, surprised.

"Yeah, 'cause you're mad."

"Well, I guess so."

"That's why I'm sorry."

I didn't know if my anger was the right reason for her to apologize, but as long as she acknowledged her mistake, it was fine by me. She said she wouldn't do it again at least.

I decided not to criticize her any further. "Okay, apology accepted."

"Really? You're not mad anymore?"

"Nope, but I might be if you do that again. Next time I say to stop, you should stop."

"All right," Jinlin agreed.

I stopped scolding her and faintly smiled. "So what happened to the fairy?"

"Oh, right," she said and opened her hand to reveal the tiny fairy.

The fairy whined with pain. It was an inhuman voice, strangely resonant. The fairy was about fifteen centimeters tall, with light, colorful clothes and wings like a dragonfly. I thought it was a female, but some types of fairy were entirely genderless, so it was hard to say for sure. But she had long hair and looked like a woman.

"Are you all right? You're not hurt, are you?" Jinlin asked.

"I'm fine! No injuries. Oh, right, I have to go!" the fairy said. She looked at Jinlin. "Thank you for saving me! I am Tilya! If we meet again, I will reward you somehow!" And with that, Tilya flew away.

"Hey, wait!" Jinlin shouted, but the fairy was too fast. She was already out of sight. Fairies didn't seem to have any strength, but they could go fast.

"Darn, she's gone. It looked like she was busy, though," I said.

Jinlin puffed out her cheeks. "I wanted to talk to her more! She could've at least repaid me somehow."

"Did you want a reward?"

"No, I just— Oh, whatever. We have to head back anyway."

"Oh? Time to go back, is it?" a woman's voice asked. "Then I won't have to drag you two back?"

The voice was a bit hoarse, and it clearly belonged to an old woman, but it exerted a unique sort of pressure. We knew who it was, but we were scared to turn around and confirm. We had to eventually, however.

After Jinlin and I looked at each other, we slowly looked behind us to see just who we expected.

"Grandmother," Jinlin mumbled with despair.

It was Pravda, and she looked furious. "Children!" she shouted, making us stand up straight. "You don't know your way around here! What are you doing running off by yourselves?! How many times do we have to tell you that it's dangerous outside the village?! We don't just mean the roads; there are threats everywhere! You could have been kidnapped! And there are lunatics who murder for fun! I only brought you along because I thought you were wiser than the average child, but you've betrayed my trust! Do you understand?!"

She continued to lecture us for a long while after that.

From her bed at the inn, Jinlin muttered, "I'm never doing anything like that again."

There were two rooms between us. My parents were in one room, and Pravda, Jinlin, and I were in the other. Pravda was already asleep, possibly exhausted from anger. At least in the end she was glad we were safe and hugged us both. My parents scolded us too, but I could tell they were already too tired by the time we got back. It was more of a brief warning than a lecture. I knew what we had done was wrong, so that was fine. But Pravda was frightening, and that was probably what made Jinlin regret it.

"I think that'd be smart," I said. "No more dangerous stuff."

"Right! I'll wait until I'm grown up for that," she declared.

"What do you mean, when you're grown up?"

"Grown-ups can go anywhere they want, right? So I'm gonna be an adventurer!"

I was surprised. "Jinlin, aren't you supposed to be the mayor? That's what your mom and dad say."

"I don't have to be the mayor right away. Besides, it's not like it *has* to be me. I have cousins who can do it."

It was true that Jinlin's parents could continue to run the village until they retired, and there was no reason her cousins couldn't take over from there. It seemed like a good idea on her part.

Still, something felt strange to me. "You don't want to be mayor?" I asked.

"It's not that I don't want to, it's that I want to be an adventurer. I want to see the world. Did you know that the things we see in picture books are actually real and out there somewhere? There's a whole bunch of interesting stuff, like waterfalls falling from islands in the sky, cities surrounded by water, and castles that disappear like mirages!"

I know those are all real now, but at the time they sounded like fairy tales. Our village had nothing so fantastical, so I couldn't believe they existed.

"Those are just dreams, Jinlin," I said. "You can't daydream all the time when you have to study to be the mayor. Anyway, we have to get up earlier tomorrow, so let's go to sleep. I'm tired." I really was terribly tired, a feeling that I haven't had in some time now.

Anyway, it took me a while to get to sleep, but before that, I heard Jinlin one more time.

"Geez, you're dumb! I'm not going to take you with me, then!" she said.

Wondering if she had plans to bring me along on her adventures, I finally fell asleep.

Chapter 3: Tragedy and Origins

"Uh, where did I leave off?"

"You stopped at when Jinlin said her dream was to become an adventurer."

"Oh, right."

Discussing events from far in the past made my mind feel kind of hazy, and I seemed to speak without thinking. It was like I lost consciousness and blacked out for a while. These were fun memories, but they were connected to painful ones, so maybe I deliberately spaced out. But this story was so ingrained in me that I could tell it without thinking.

This tale was on its way to devastation. I didn't want to remember it.

The next morning, we had to get ready to leave, so we didn't have any time to go sightseeing before we departed for home. I woke up at the inn, had breakfast with Jinlin and Pravda, and headed to the loading dock. My parents were there already. They had gone to bed before us because they needed to be there early to get some work done. They assessed the sales value of the goods they had unloaded yesterday, and they also packed the necessities we were taking back to Hathara. We were the last bit of luggage to be stuffed inside, after which the horse would be whipped and the carriage would leave.

"Rentt, Jinlin, we're about to go. Get on," Pravda said.

We nodded and boarded the carriage. We acted like knights given orders by their superior, in large part due to Pravda's lecture the day prior. Neither of us wanted her to snap at us like that again. We were so quick that the carriage was ready to leave quite early.

"Let's go, then," my father said from the coachman's seat. "Ready?"

We were all already on board, as was the luggage. "Yes, no problems here," my mother said. "Go."

My father whipped the horse, and the carriage slowly began to roll. It was a short visit, but it turned out to be a big adventure for me and Jinlin. We did almost get badly hurt, but we got to meet a fairy, which was more than enough adventure for a child. Now that I'm an adventurer, I know just how rare fairies are. On the road back, Pravda told me fairies were rare, but I only thought they were rare in the way saria flowers were. Saria flowers, by the way, are seasonal flowers in Hathara that only bloom under a full moon. They're fairly uncommon, but if you want to harvest them, you can collect plenty. Fairies, on the other hand, are hard to come by.

Jinlin wanted to brag about our trip to Jal and Dol the minute we got back to the village. I did too, to some degree. As hesitant as I had been, when I thought back to our little excursion, I had to admit it was fun. I wouldn't have bragged, but I did want to tell them about what had happened in town and about Jinlin's big adventure and her big failure. That's all to say that the journey back home was fun and I had a lot to look forward to. Up to a point, at least.

"You helped a fairy? That's why you put yourself in such danger?" Pravda asked.

The carriage rocked back and forth as we explained the events in the village. She was surprised, of course. I was trembling in fear, afraid she would get angry again, but Jinlin acted like there was nothing to worry about. Maybe she was just used to making Pravda angry, or maybe she was naturally brave. It was probably both.

"Yeah, I mean, it kept asking for help," Jinlin argued.

"Fairies are an extremely rare sight. Seeing one during your first time away from the village is quite an experience," Pravda said in awe. "Maybe you're loved by one of the stars. Well, never mind that. If either of you happen to find a fairy again, you must stay away."

"You mean because it's dangerous?" I asked, surprised by her command.

Pravda shook her head. "No, not that. Well, there's that too, but more importantly, you shouldn't simply approach a fairy. Their way of thinking is fundamentally different from ours. You never know what they might do. Of course, not all fairies are like this and I don't speak for all of them, but did nothing seem strange to you about this fairy?"

Jinlin and I looked at each other. Then I remembered that maybe something was a little odd. It hadn't seemed interested in speaking with us and had expressed no concerned for our safety. Maybe that was because it thought differently from humans.

"Anything come to mind?" Pravda asked again.

Jinlin seemed to come to the same conclusion I did. We silently acknowledged that we had thought of something.

"Falling from a tree wasn't the only danger you placed yourselves in, is what I'm saying. You don't want to be swapped with changelings, do you?"

We recalled when our parents and cousins warned us that if we did anything bad, we would be replaced by changelings. They never said who would do that, though.

"Is that something fairies do?" Jinlin asked.

"Yes," Pravda said. "When nobody is watching, fairies switch places with human children. It's a habit they have. To us, swapping your own children with someone else's, one from another species at that, would be unthinkable. But this is what I mean when I say they don't think like us. They have trouble understanding humans."

As the carriage moved onward, Jinlin and I got far more used to the rocking than we were yesterday. Jinlin seemed prone to motion sickness, so she would never fully get accustomed to it, but Pravda had bought medicine for that in town and gave it to her before we left. She gave me some too, but I was fine anyway, so maybe I didn't need to take it. The medicine was extremely bitter and painful to consume, but the motion sickness was even worse than that for Jinlin, so she didn't think twice about gulping it down. But some time after we talked about fairies, the medicine made us sleepy. We were told it might make us a bit tired, and I remember realizing that the medicine must have caused it. I could make myself stay awake, but there was no reason not to sleep. My mother and Pravda were still awake anyway. I gave in and let myself fall into the world of dreams.

I woke to the sound of a loud crash, clueless as to how long it had been. I felt like I had been tossed into the air, and then everything flipped upside down around me. I was unable to look around, but I found the whole incident fascinating. I vividly remember the fruit floating in the air. I remember the way the grass looked. I could almost paint a picture of it.

Time moved dreadfully slow, but the real dread soon began to set in. I had no idea what had happened. By the time I realized that the carriage had probably toppled over, all the luggage had scattered in a chaotic mess. I had been slammed against the wooden boxes and the sides of the carriage, and severe pains rushed through me when I tried to move.

Desperate to see what had happened to the others, I observed my surroundings. I looked for Jinlin first. My parents and Pravda had seemed invincible at the time, but not her. She always came off like I could have lost her at any time, so I worried excessively about her. Luckily, I found her easily enough. She was underneath some boxes, but she was still breathing.

"Uhn, Rentt," she groaned.

Thankfully, there was nothing too heavy in the boxes, so even a child like me could move them aside with some effort. She wasn't unharmed, but she managed to stand up by herself.

"Jinlin! Are you all right?! Can you walk?" I immediately asked.

"Yeah, I'm fine," she said. Cold sweat was pouring down her face. "Where are the adults?"

That was the first time I asked that question myself. Not that I forgot about them, but it was strange they hadn't come to look for us. We were children, and the adults were constantly concerned for our well-being. If there was a huge accident, like say a carriage turning over, the first thing they would have done was find us.

We couldn't have ended up that far apart either. They'd only need to search around the carriage.

When I realized they hadn't come, I felt uneasy. Severely uneasy. Jinlin seemed to feel the same way.

Just when I could hardly sit still anymore, a loud boom came from past the carriage. Shocked, I turned in that direction and saw a pillar of flame. I had no idea what it was at the time, but Jinlin did.

"Magic?!" she gasped and ran toward it. I followed behind her.

What we saw stunned us both. It's hard to describe, but it looked sinister, to say the least. It looked like a big, silver wolf, but its eyes were bloodshot and its massive body was surrounded by a wavering wicked black aura. It appeared to have a thirst for carnage. It was like destruction incarnate, or an apostle of Hell.

We also saw Pravda holding a staff. She was the one who had cast the magic. I didn't know she could use magic, but Jinlin did. Maybe Pravda had taught her some to use in case of emergencies.

Pravda noticed us and turned around. "You two?! You're alive?! Run away! I'll keep this monster from—"

Those were her last words. Before I even knew what had happened, the wolf's claws were sticking out of her back. Pravda coughed up blood, and the light disappeared from her eyes. And then she was dead.

I had seen corpses before, but this was the first time I witnessed the moment of death. I was unable to think for a moment. But then I remembered that I had to run. I grabbed Jinlin's hand and tried to get as far from the wolf as I could.

"Rentt?! Rentt, what about Grandmother?!" Jinlin screamed, her voice lacking emotion.

I knew what she wanted to say, of course, but Pravda was already gone. We had to survive, so we had to run. There was nothing more to be done.

"What about your parents?!" Jinlin continued, figuring they had to be somewhere around here.

Jinlin was likely much more confused than I was. She must not have seen the other two corpses by the wolf, but I had. We were the only survivors.

Maybe I was somewhat heartless. It would have been normal to freeze up in that situation, just as Jinlin was doing. But I refused to let her die.

I ran. I ran to survive. I ran to make it back home. I ran to protect my childhood friend.

I don't know how long we ran for. "This has to be far enough," I murmured between heavy breaths, far from the overturned carriage. But then Jinlin stammered my name, her voice shaky, and she pointed straight ahead.

It's so obvious what was there that I don't feel I need to explain, but it was that vile wolf. Its bloodshot eyes callously looked at us. In hindsight, it was strange that a child could run so far from that monster. The wolf had to be playing with us. It could have killed us in an instant, but it wanted to see how far we would flee. Now playtime was over. I hadn't caught a single glimpse of it while we were running, so if it was showing itself now, it must have gotten bored.

I didn't understand that at the time and thought I had to keep running. Unfortunately, my legs wouldn't listen to me. Jinlin didn't seem like she could walk one more step either. We were cornered.

I don't know what came over me, but I trudged toward the wolf and stood before it. It wasn't the smartest decision, and it was probably pointless, but it was all I could do to protect Jinlin. It was all I could do to save her life. I thought she could run away while the wolf killed me.

But the wolf was watching us. It knew there was no way we could escape. It didn't matter if I sacrificed myself, but I didn't know that.

I spread my arms and stared at the wolf. "Jinlin, run," I urged. "Leave the monster to me."

Jinlin shook her head. "No, Rentt! I, I—"

"Just run! I'll hold it back!"

We argued for a while until the wolf finally got fed up. It sighed and raised its front leg. Slowly, it extended its sharp claws, the blood of Pravda and my parents still coating them. They had been stabbed and torn apart by these claws. In a few seconds, the same would happen to me. But if I could buy enough time for Jinlin to escape, that was enough. With that in mind, I felt self-assured as I stood there.

I closed my eyes and felt a gust of wind as the wolf swung its front leg down. But then something pushed me over. The claws never hit me. Wondering what happened, I opened my eyes. What I found was the worst conclusion I could have imagined and the last thing I wanted to see.

Jinlin whispered my name, blood dripping from her mouth. I looked further down and saw a sharp claw jutting from her chest. It was supposed to impale me, but Jinlin took my place. The wolf slowly pulled its claw out, and blood fountained from Jinlin's body. She fell to the ground in a crimson puddle.

"Jinlin! Jinlin! Hey! Jinlin!" I shouted as I ran up to her. I didn't care about the wolf anymore. I didn't care if it killed me. Jinlin was more important. I had to save her somehow. But the blood kept pouring out, and she was turning paler by the second. I tried to think of some way to keep her alive, but it was futile.

She could still talk, but her voice was faint and slow. "Rentt, I'm sorry, I'm—"

"Jinlin, don't talk! You'll die, you're going to die!"

"Tell my parents that I'm sorry. Live on, Rentt. Before I die, I want you to know that I wanted to, um, marry you one day."

"We can do that, Jinlin. You just have to survive."

"Oh, Rentt," she said, laughing, "you can live happily with someone else."

Death happens all too fast. Jinlin's body rapidly went limp, and soon enough, she no longer responded to my words.

"Jinlin, Jinlin! Why?!" I cried. I didn't care about anything anymore. I couldn't even deliver her message because that wolf monster was still there. Something in me snapped and I picked up a stick to face off against the wolf. It was foolish. There was no way I could win, and my chance of survival was even lower than if I tried to run. But if I was going to die, I wanted to die fighting.

The wolf stared at me with amusement and then straightened out and faced me like a beast hunting prey. That was when I realized that it had been playing games before. I still don't know why it felt the need to take a fighting stance, but maybe the wolf thought it was the proper thing to do. Now that I think about it, the wolf was on guard against Pravda as well. I'd have to ask the monster itself to know for sure, though.

I brandished my stick. My form was dreadful, and I could only run at a plodding pace. This was no way to combat a monster. But it didn't matter. I wasn't trying to fight so much as trying to die. I don't know if the wolf knew that or not, but it looked entertained as it opened its mouth wide and approached me. It looked like it was going to chomp me in half, but I wasn't afraid.

Its mouth came closer. If I attacked its gaping maw, I thought I might be able to do some damage, even with a stick. I stabbed at it and, surprisingly, I managed to scrape its gums a bit. I don't know if it was a fluke, or the wolf wasn't paying attention, or it let it happen on purpose, but I was satisfied. At least I got back at it somehow.

Accepting my fate, I waited to be crushed in its jaws. But just then, I heard a loud clang. Something defended me from the wolf's teeth.

I looked up and saw an adult man. He held a broadsword far larger than my entire body, and he was using it to keep the wolf at bay.

"Stand back," he said, restraining his anger, "I'll do something about this."

I was too distraught to think, so I did as I was told. The wolf tried to claw at me, but the man swung his broadsword and forced it to back away. Even now, I still think he was an outstanding fighter. At the time, I knew nothing of combat, but I could tell at a glance that he was a master thanks to his beautiful motions.

This led into a battle between man and wolf. The wolf leaped at the man, and the man flailed his sword at the wolf. Both moved too fast for me to follow. I could see how much the wolf had been holding back against me, and I came to understand how talented the man was. It was like the battle took place in its own world. Both were evenly matched. The wolf avoided the sword by a hair's breadth or blocked it with its fangs. The man deflected the wolf's claws and fangs with his broadsword or dodged faster than the eye could see.

When they both finally reached the limits of their stamina, the man achieved victory. The wolf let its guard down for only an instant, and the man got right up next to it and delivered a blow that left a gash in the wolf's chest. The wolf howled in pain. It swung a front leg at the man and knocked him away, but the man blocked the desperate attack with his sword and made it out unscathed.

Dark blood dripped from the wolf's chest, forming a lake of red. Its breath grew ragged, and its eyes, filled with nothing but the desire to kill, searched around frantically. I was far from the scene, but I still recoiled. The man, however, was unfazed.

The wolf and the man glowered at each other for a while longer until the tension broke and the wolf backed off. Then, to my surprise, the wolf ran far away. I watched it all play out from nearby, and I was dumbfounded. The wolf never seemed like the type to flee, but it did just that in the face of the man.

The man remained on guard for a while, but when its sinister presence could no longer be felt, he ran up to me. "Are you all right?!" he asked.

I had been saved at the last second from a monster attack. His question was only natural, but I wasn't in the right state of mind.

"Why?" I asked back.

"Hm?"

"Why didn't you come sooner?!"

It was the worst way I could have responded. If I were to save someone and they said the same to me now, it would be like a nightmare. I should have thanked him. I knew that. But when I looked at Jinlin's corpse lying at my feet, I couldn't say anything else.

Still, the man was kind. He looked at my dead friend. "Sorry. If only I ran a bit faster. I'm so sorry. It's my fault."

I couldn't blame him. The truth was that they just got unlucky. Jinlin did, my parents did, and Pravda did. Only I was lucky enough to escape that powerful monster with my life. And it was thanks to this man, so I had no right to complain.

But the man still apologized. He wiped the tears from my eyes and then gave me a hug. It only made me cry and scream louder.

"Are you done?" The man asked after I had bawled my eyes out.

"Yeah, sorry about that," I said. I still didn't feel better, but I had cooled off a bit. I was depressed and didn't know what to do, and my mind was still muddled, but I had come to realize that I couldn't blame the man for anything.

"No, you did well," the man said. "Not because you apologized but because you were able to stand up to that beast despite your young age. Anyway, uh, about your deceased companions…"

"I'd like to carry them back to the village, but I don't think I can," I said.

The dead needed to be mourned, but at times like these, it was standard to leave the bodies in the wild for monsters or animals to eat. It was hard to transport bodies, and they could also attract monsters, making matters worse. I didn't know these details back then, but I knew there was no getting them back to the village without a vehicle.

"No, it's not impossible," the man said. "Where should they be taken? Is it a village around here? Hathara, Alga, or Mul?" Those were all nearby villages, so the man must have been familiar with the territory.

"Yes, Hathara. I was on my way back there," I replied.

"I see. How tragic."

"Never mind that, what do you mean it's not impossible?"

"Oh, I came here by carriage, you see. I sensed that monster's mana and came running all this way, but if you wait another half a day, the carriage should get here. It can take the bodies back. Thankfully I reserved the carriage so there'd be no passengers besides the coachman and myself."

I didn't entirely understand what the man was talking about at the time, but thinking about it now, he must have run half a day's distance by carriage entirely on foot. He somehow sensed the monster's presence from that far away. Plus, he went out of his way to reserve a carriage that was traveling through an unpopulated rural area. Thinking about it rationally, he was highly suspicious and bizarre, but he did save me, so he had my full trust.

"So they wouldn't mind taking all the bodies?" I asked.

"Sure. I know the coachman personally, actually. I can ask for a little extra service. We'll have to wait here until the carriage arrives, so I think I'll use this time to get all the bodies together in one place. If they had any precious items to keep as heirlooms, you'll need to gather those up yourself. I wouldn't know what they valued. There's an important job for you to do."

Most likely, the man gave me that job out of kindness. He wanted to distract me with something. I don't know how much it helped. Maybe a little bit.

"Oh, hey, here we go. He's here, Rentt," the man said as he put a hand to his forehead and looked beyond the bonfire. The sun had long since set and he had just said that the carriage might not arrive until tomorrow, so he was delighted to see it coming.

As for me, I was in the mood to go wander around the forest until I was killed by monsters, but talking to the man was starting to make me feel better. He was a good storyteller, and he picked out stories that children would like. He spoke of a distant land of earth and trees, of a ship that flew in the sky, of a fool who tried to take the sun's place, and of the origin and final destination of the human soul.

I asked the man who he was and why he knew so much.

He thought about it for a bit before he answered. "I'm an adventurer," he said. "A Mithril-class adventurer. The name's Wilfried Rucker."

At the time, I wasn't especially surprised to hear that. I knew of adventurers but not their specific ranks. I noted that this man was what Jinlin had hoped to become one day and that she would've been happy to meet him, but that was all. Now that I really think about it, though, maybe that was the moment something took root in my subconscious. Jinlin could never become an adventurer now, but I survived, so I felt I had to achieve her dream in her place.

"Wilfried, I spent this whole time wondering why you suddenly jumped out of the carriage and ran off. What happened here?" the coachman asked after he got off the carriage. He was a pleasant young man with long hair and an odd air about him. He was strangely pretty for a man, and he seemed out of place for a coachman in the countryside. Thinking about it now, he would have been a better fit as a noble or a priest.

"Well, I'll tell you about it later," Wilfried said. "Anyway, I want to take these bodies back to their village. You mind?"

Most coachmen would have objected, but the man nodded. "I suppose I don't. I don't have any coffins, but there's enough cloth to wrap them up. Might as well."

He went back to the carriage and then returned with tons of cloth. It looked expensive, worth a fortune if sold as fabric, but the man thought nothing of it and used it to wrap up the corpses. He did so gently, too. It was undoubtedly good luck that I met these two.

Once they were all wrapped in cloth and brought to the carriage, Wilfried introduced me to the coachman.

"This is Azel. Azel Goth. He's a traveling merchant but without any route to follow. He's sort of a gadabout. Sometimes I hire him when he's got the time. He also does some adventuring on the side, so he's good for forming an adventuring party."

"I'm Azel, nice to meet you. And you are?"

"Rentt," I said tersely.

"I see, got it," Azel replied. "The sun has set for the day, so I think we should head to your village tomorrow. Does that sound good to you?"

It wasn't like I could complain. I could have tried to go home alone, but not with all the bodies, so I had to do what they said.

"That would be fine. Thank you," I said.

"It's nothing," Azel answered with a smile. "You should get some rest for the day. Wilfried and I will keep watch." He stroked my head.

His voice was so kind and compassionate that just hearing it made me sleepy. Some time later, my eyelids grew heavy and I fell asleep.

The next morning we immediately set off for the village. We reached Hathara that night. The villagers were surprised to see the unfamiliar carriage, but they were even more startled when I got off it. They wondered what had happened to the carriage we had left on, but I suspect most of the adults had a good guess.

Wilfried and Azel explained the situation to the mayor and his wife right away. The village children asked me some questions, but I couldn't work up the will to answer them. I knew I should have said something, but I couldn't even accept the facts, let alone relay them.

What happened after that felt like it went by in a flash. The deaths of my parents, Pravda, and Jinlin were announced and a funeral was held. I was adopted into the mayor's family. This happened over the course of three days, and to my surprise, Wilfried and Azel stayed in the village that whole time. When I asked Ingo about it later, he said it was because they were worried about me.

They wanted someone to look after me because it looked like I might hurt myself, but the villagers were busy with the funeral. If nobody had been around, I likely would have had the urge to die, so they were probably correct. It was a terrible way to feel after they'd saved my life, but that was just how much the tragedy impacted me.

Part of their reason for staying was also because the villagers wanted more people around to help with the burial. The adventurers turned out to be a great help. Offerings had to be gathered from the forest for the funeral, but they were quick to collect enough. They were great people.

Once the funeral and the administrative proceedings were over with, I finally faced reality. It was nothing but pain. I didn't know what to do next. I was the mayor's son now, so maybe I should have aimed to become the mayor. But Jinlin had said she wanted to be an adventurer and see the world. Her dream could never come true, but I could still achieve it in her stead. From a more rational perspective, maybe that wasn't the best way to think about it. But that was my idea, so I asked the nearest adventurer for help.

"An adventurer? Why?" Wilfried said when I asked him how to become an adventurer. It was the obvious response.

"Because Jinlin, my friend, said she wanted to become an adventurer one day," I answered.

Wilfried seemed to have assumed as much already. "She was the one who passed away?" he asked, just to be sure.

"Yeah."

"I see."

Wilfried closed his eyes to think for a bit. He was silent for a painfully long time. I thought he might tell me I was wrong to feel this way. At the very least, telling the other villagers that I wanted to be an adventurer wouldn't have been well-received. There were more than a few children who said they would be adventurers, and I could always tell that the adults thought they'd be better off if they weren't. Adventurers were mostly ruffians, so they looked down on the profession. But more importantly, the citizens of Hathara knew that adventuring was a dangerous job with a great risk of death. When I first told the adults in the village that I wanted to be an adventurer, most of them told me not to.

Wilfried finished thinking and opened his eyes. "I won't tell you not to try, but first, you'll have to train," he said matter-of-factly. "To begin with, you can't register with a guild until you're fifteen. You've got a decade left to wait, and you need to learn how to fight monsters by then."

It was a more practical response than I was expecting. When a five-year-old tells you they want to be an adventurer, you usually wouldn't respond that way. No matter how favorably you viewed adventurers, you'd normally tell them to try their best and leave it at that. But Wilfried was different.

"Also, you need knowledge," Wilfried continued. "Learning to read and write is the bare minimum. Otherwise you'll be deceived for sure. Learn math too, for the same reason. Knowledge of medicinal herbs and other plants, of monster types and their attributes, and of wilderness survival skills are also crucial. Hathara is a small village, but I've met the old medicine woman, and the mayor owns some books. There's plenty of knowledge to be found here. If you insist on becoming an adventurer, I'd start by convincing them to teach you."

This detailed advice was actually extremely helpful. "If I do all that, can I become a great adventurer?" I asked.

"Can't say for sure. That'd just put you at the starting line. Whatever happens next depends on how much effort you put in. If you want to try, though, do what I said. You should at least be able to walk on your own two feet. Just don't die till your dreams are realized," he said sincerely.

He must have known that if I kept living without any goals, I'd one day wander off into the forest to die. Even a reckless goal would keep me alive as long as I kept pushing toward it. I assume that was why he took me seriously. I didn't know that back then, but I did know he was speaking to me in earnest.

I nodded. "All right, I'll try."

The funeral was over and I was officially adopted by the mayor. Now that the village had settled down, it was time for Wilfried and Azel to leave.

"Rentt, if you become a powerful adventurer, come see me sometime," Wilfried told me before we parted. "I honestly can't tell you where I'll be in ten years, but if I'm still alive, I'll still be adventuring somewhere. I can treat you to a beer or something." He rubbed my head.

"Ideally, I'll have my own shop by then," Azel said. "If you ever hear about my company, come give it a visit. I'll probably name it the Goth Company. Assuming I ever have one." His tone made it hard to tell if he was serious or kidding.

The goal of most traveling merchants was to set up their own store, so it wasn't that strange, but Wilfried looked appalled. "That'll never happen if you keep screwing around," he said. "Rentt, he's not going to get there in ten years. It'll be a lot quicker to come find me."

That was the last thing they told me before they left. After that, my new life began. Before this, I had spent all my free time playing in the house. Sometimes Jinlin would invite me over to climb trees or play with toy swords, but that was all I ever did outside. Now, however, I had a specific objective: become an adventurer because Jinlin couldn't. That wasn't all, of course. On some level, I must have wanted to slay that monster that ran away. The wicked wolf that killed Jinlin and my parents. I wouldn't say it was about revenge, but that wolf symbolized the tragedy. It was something I wanted to overcome. Wilfried could match the wolf, and he said he was Mithril-class, so that was when I began my journey to become a Mithril-class adventurer. No matter what it took, I swore I would get there one day.

I started my training, but first I had to ask someone to teach me some skills. I asked my foster parents to teach me math, reading, and writing, and I asked the hunters to teach me to use hunting knives and bows. I also asked the craftsmen to teach me some things, and I asked the medicine woman for lessons on how to tell plants apart, how to make medicine, and what the different types of monsters were. At first they were all confounded by my requests, but after I asked a few dozen times, they gave in. By the end, they were all happy to teach me. I was so desperate to succeed that I never skipped a lesson, and I practiced thoroughly, so maybe my teachers enjoyed it too.

"I spent the next decade like that, making myself into the Rentt Faina you know today. And that's pretty much it," I said, concluding my story.

"You've been trying to reach Mithril-class all this time because of that?" Lorraine asked.

I never hesitated to tell anyone that my goal was to become a Mithril-class adventurer, but I never told anyone the reasons either, so this was naturally the first time Lorraine had heard about it. It wasn't that I didn't want to talk about it, but it was a difficult topic to discuss. It took a long time too.

I seldom talked about the misfortune in my life. All adventurers had some tragic stories, but rather than tell them, we preferred to pass the time enjoying food and drinks. It wasn't that we forgot our own tragedies or found them meaningless. They were important to us and helped shape who we were. But they were hard to bring up among others, and we didn't want to dampen the mood. We were trying to forget our troubles by drinking with friends, so nobody wanted to dredge up their past suffering.

Regardless, I told Lorraine all about it today because I felt like it.

I looked up at the sky and saw the stars twinkle. The sky was darker in Maalt, and there were fewer stars. They used fire and magic lamps to light up the city at night, which obscured the lights in the sky. Hathara was hardly lit by anything. They had a bonfire going in the center of the village tonight, but the stars were still visible.

"But even with all that effort, I've never been anything more than Bronze-class. You can't always get what you want," I said.

"That's been true so far," Lorraine replied, "but you don't know what the future will bring."

She was right. Maybe this was hubris, but I felt I could really make it to Mithril-class now. It was still quite possible, however, that I'd come to a standstill again. More than likely, in fact. I just didn't know where the ceiling would be yet. I'd felt the same way when I was young, so I knew better than to get my hopes up too high. I just planned to do everything I could.

"By the way, you say that monster could fight on equal footing with a Mithril-class adventurer? Are there a lot of monsters that powerful around here?" Lorraine asked. It was a good question, considering that if there were, we wouldn't be able to casually have this banquet.

"No, not that I know of. That was the only time I ever saw one. I've never seen a monster like that anywhere else, actually. I've read monster guides but couldn't find it listed. I'm pretty sure I asked you if you'd heard of this monster before too. A wolf far larger than a human, shrouded in darkness."

"Yes, I believe you did, quite a while ago. Though, I didn't know what prompted that question. I said it might be a ze'ev gadol, a garm, or mawiang, I think?"

"Right. I'm surprised you remember. None of those suggestions were right, though."

I had looked up all of the monsters Lorraine mentioned, but none of them were the wolf I saw. They were different sizes or shapes, and they didn't have the dark aura. Not all monsters had been identified, so it was to be expected, but failing to find a single clue was a bit disappointing.

"Maybe it was some new breed, or a unique monster," Lorraine speculated. "That would make it hard to find, I suppose. Maybe nobody else has ever seen it, or maybe everyone who did has been permanently silenced. Maybe that Mithril-class adventurer knows something about it."

"Wilfried? I wonder where he is now."

"Did you never go pay him a visit?"

"No, I haven't seen him since then. I tried to find him a few times, but he doesn't seem to be anywhere in the country. He must have gone to another nation. I thought it'd be lame to go find him until I climbed the ranks a little more."

"And then you were stuck at the same rank for ten years."

"Yeah, well, yes."

Lorraine was correct, as pitiful as that was. It wasn't just about my pride, though. If I wasn't at least Silver- or Gold-class, traveling would be brutal. It would be different if I had a party, but I'd be going solo. Hardly anyone would even hire a solo Bronze-class adventurer as a bodyguard for international travel. But that changed when you were Silver-class.

"Then what about that company?" Lorraine asked. "The one Azel said he would start. The Goth Company?"

"There's no company with that name in this country; as far as I know, anyway. Either he's still a traveling merchant, he went to a different country, or he started a company under a different name."

Judging by his personality, he was most likely still a traveling merchant, but there was no way to know for sure. He could very well have been working in another country. The Kingdom of Yaaran was a small and insignificant nation, so it wasn't the best place to make money. Their reason for coming to this area wasn't to sell wares but presumably something else. They came from the western nations, but Mithril-class adventurers operated all around the world. That information didn't help much, but maybe it was worth trying to find them at some point. There was at least a slight chance they would know something.

"Considering they suggested you come see them again, they certainly made it hard to find them," Lorraine muttered.

But that was the way adventurers were. Azel was also a traveling merchant, which meant he wouldn't stay in any one place anyway. It was to be expected.

"Well, he's Mithril-class, so he could be surprisingly easy to find if I try. Maybe."

"Isn't it the opposite? Information about Mithril-class adventurers is sometimes restricted by governments."

In that case, we were both right. Mithril-class adventurers came in all sorts. Some stood out and drew attention, while others were thoroughly secretive.

"Well, I'll work on finding them at some point. I wanted to become human again first, but that may never happen, so I think I'll seek them out while I figure out how to change back."

Lorraine sighed. "I feel like you just keep giving yourself more to do. Will you be all right?"

"I hardly need to sleep, so I've got plenty of time. I don't think I'm overworking myself just yet. Anyway, it's not like I have to solve either of these things right away. I'll take my time," I replied with a wry smile.

"I could argue with you, but I don't think you'll listen. Do what you will for now, but pay attention to me when times get tough. Everyone has limits," Lorraine concluded.

We stood up to go back to the bonfire. "Oh, there you are," someone said from behind us before we could leave. "Rentt and, hm, I believe your name was Lorraine?"

We turned around and saw an impish old lady with a malicious smile. I knew who it was, of course. It was Gharb, the village's medicine woman. She was my foster grandmother's younger sister, so my great aunt, I suppose. She also taught me all about medicine.

"Teacher, why are you here?" I asked.

"You haven't called me that in ages. Well, in any case, why do you think I'm here? We're holding a banquet for you, and it's not terribly exciting if the guest of honor's not present. I was planning to stay at home because parties aren't good for these old bones, but Ingo dragged me out, and now he's making me run these errands for him. Good grief," Gharb complained. She looked perfectly healthy, though, and I was certain she was lying.

Now that I had enhanced mana and was this close to her, it was easy to tell that she was a magician. That she hid it so well throughout our lessons was shocking. Not that she ever needed to use magic in the village, so I guess it wasn't that difficult to hide. You'd need your own equivalent mana to detect the mana of another, after all.

But she did teach me plenty of general knowledge about magic, so I should have suspected as much.

"Oh, you noticed?" Gharb asked in response to my gaze. "You had but a drop of mana when you left the village, but you seem to have quite a bit now. Is that thanks to this Lorraine girl, perhaps?"

If I could see her mana, then it stood to reason that she could see mine. That she could estimate how much mana I had at a glance, however, demonstrated that she was a highly capable magician. Lorraine seemed to come to the same conclusion, judging by the mild shock in her expression.

"I guess I should introduce myself. I'm Lorraine Vivie, and yes, I have been teaching Rentt a bit of magic."

Gharb cackled in response. "I'm Gharb Faina, Rentt's great aunt. I taught him about medicine. And I don't go around publicizing this, but I'm a magician as well. None of the villagers know that aside from Ingo."

"Doesn't Fahri know too? She said she was your disciple," Lorraine said.

Gharb looked shocked. "How many times have I told her to keep that a secret? Well, I knew she had loose lips. I also told her that she didn't have to go out of her way to hide it, so perhaps that has something to do with it. You're a magician too, so maybe she thought it was hopeless to try. Riri knows too then, I take it?"

"Yes, but if you really want to keep it a secret, it doesn't seem like you're trying very hard."

"Oh, it hardly matters in this day and age. Back in my day, this village was far more savage. I had no choice but to hide it. But times have changed. When I decided to teach Fahri, I knew I'd be exposed eventually."

I didn't know there was ever a time the village was the way she claimed. If it was when Gharb was young, though, it would have to have been at least fifty years ago. I wanted to ask why it had been so savage, but Gharb continued speaking before I had the chance.

"Well, enough about that. Head back to the banquet soon. You too, Lorraine. They want to see that illusion magic again. I didn't get to watch it myself, so I'd love to get the opportunity."

"I don't mind, but it seems to me that you could use it too," Lorraine pointed out based on an estimation of Gharb's magic power.

Gharb shook her head. "No, certainly not. I sensed the mana from when you used it, and I'm too old for anything so complex and demanding of energy," she said. Then she headed back the way she came.

"Wait, Teacher," I called out when something occurred to me. "I want to ask about something."

Gharb stopped and turned around. "What?"

"Wasn't there a shrine in this village? Is it still around?"

That was the point of this journey in the first place. I was planning to give it a look tomorrow, after today's greetings were done, but I thought it might be worth asking this village's living encyclopedia about the shrine's history.

"You mean the one near Ingo's house?" she asked.

"No, not that one. You know the run-down house out west? The one behind that."

As soon as I said it, Gharb's face clouded. But it was only for a moment, and I wouldn't have noticed were I not paying attention.

"There's a shrine there?" she quickly replied.

She probably knew about it, so maybe she was playing dumb. I didn't see why she would, though. It was a small, abandoned shrine. I had repaired it, but it was still nothing that stood out. Its location in particular kept it from notice. If I hadn't found it, it might have been completely destroyed at some point. I had no idea what secrets it may have held.

"There is one, yeah," I responded. "I fixed it up a long time ago."

"Is that the source of your divinity? I see," Gharb said, picking up on that immediately. There had been little time between my obtaining divinity and my leaving the village, so I'd never even told Gharb about it. But if she didn't have divinity, she wouldn't have been able to see it. I assumed that meant Gharb possessed divinity herself.

She seemed to understand what I was thinking. "I don't have any divinity of my own, but sometimes, when you would come back to visit, I happened to see you do something to our food reserves. I figured you were using divinity."

I knew what she was talking about, but I was surprised she was so sharp as to notice it.

"Rentt, what were you doing to the food reserves?" Lorraine wondered.

"Oh, well, some of it was always close to rotting, but purifying food with divinity helps it last longer. It also stops stuff from fermenting though, so you can't do it with some food."

For example, purifying leafy vegetables could keep them fresh in even warm temperatures for up to a month. Normally, they would only last one or two weeks no matter how they were preserved. But foods that had to ferment, such as pickled vegetables or alcohol, would not ferment if they were purified. It would work if you wanted to end the fermentation process at whichever state you preferred, but if the intent was preservation, there was no sense in using purification. As such, I made a distinction between what I purified and what I didn't. I could do this even when I had little divinity, so it was an ability I treasured. I couldn't use it at all in battle, however, and I couldn't even purge undead monsters. I only used it on water or food.

"I feel like that's a horrific waste of divinity," Lorraine grumbled.

"It's not like I was going to run out, so why not?" I responded. "Besides, shouldn't holy power be used for peaceful applications?" I did actually run low on divinity, but it recovered after I slept, so it wasn't a big deal.

"You can use your divinity however you choose, so I don't particularly mind, but is there anyone else who uses it that way? When did you realize you could do that in the first place?"

"When I first found out I could use divinity, I tested a few things out. I tried it on food, water, plants, humans, all kinds of stuff, but not much was visibly affected. I think that was mostly because I had little divinity at the time, but for simple effects like delaying the expiration of food, there was plenty more I could do with it. So much that naming it all would be a pain."

I tried just about anything I could when it came to the degradation of objects, and I'd learned that I could delay it for most of them, including food. That was why it would take ages to list everything.

"I feel like if you tried it now, you might get some interesting results," Lorraine said, excited to experiment.

I knew how she felt, considering that I could now purify ash and make grass grow from it. I wondered if I could cause plants to sprout from food now too. It would be unnecessary, so ideally not. But I'd never know until I tried. I decided to give it a go later.

"Well now, when I heard Rentt finally brought a young lass to the village, I was wondering what she was like," Gharb said, looking stunned. "You're unbelievably similar, right down to the way you think and the things you do, from the sound of it."

"Are we?" I asked. "I guess we do get along pretty well."

Lorraine added, "Rentt is never surprised by anything I do. Rather, he's willing to cooperate, so it's nice to have him around. Maybe we are similar after all. In that we're both meticulous about our research, especially."

It wasn't wrong to call me meticulous, but Lorraine bordered on obsessive. As far as cooperating, even now I was assisting her with research into monsters and their Existential Evolution. Lorraine was never shocked and focused on facts first, so I found it nice to have her around as well.

"Hm, is that right?" Gharb asked. "Rentt was always curious about the strangest things. Like that shrine. You repaired it at some point, didn't you?"

"You told me to go find some herbs, so I went walking around the village and the forest and stumbled upon it. Somehow I memorized where it was. Then later on, shortly before I left for Maalt, I wanted to do something to pay back the village."

"So you fixed up that shrine? You could have done the one by Ingo's house instead."

There was a shrine near the mayor's house as well, but unlike the one I repaired, it was fairly large and already well-maintained. The village craftsmen took care of it, and they were far more skilled than me. There was no need for me to get involved there.

"How could I do that? The one I repaired was small enough that it seemed manageable, is all. Besides, well, I didn't think anyone would get mad if I messed up with that one," I admitted.

To be honest, the latter of those two points might have been more important. There was the slight possibility that I could have been cursed. But the other shrine had been ignored for ages and hadn't cursed the village, so I decided that one would be fine.

In the end, I had successfully repaired the shrine, and I had even been granted divinity for it, so it had all worked out swimmingly.

"I don't know if I should call you thoughtful or cowardly. Well, now I get it. So, you want to know if that shrine is still there?"

"Yeah, what happened to it?"

I was a bit concerned that it had been destroyed. I didn't think the villagers would have done that, but the shrine was behind an abandoned house deep in the trees on the edge of the village, so I feared that animals or monsters might have encountered it. If so, I was planning to repair it again as thanks for receiving the gift of divinity, but it would be highly preferable if it were still intact.

"Nobody goes there, including myself, so I honestly couldn't tell you," Gharb answered. "How about you go give it a look tomorrow, while the sun is still out?"

Gharb seemed like she knew something, so I was disappointed to hear that. But I had decided to go see it for myself anyway, so I didn't mind.

"All right, I'll do that," I replied.

"Oh, and after you do that, come over to my house. Maybe we'll have something to talk about," Gharb said. Then she finally turned around and walked away.

"Do you think she's going to tell us something?" Lorraine asked.

"I don't know about that, but she's always been tough to figure out."

We talked until we remembered that they wanted us back at the banquet, so we headed toward the bonfire.

We returned to the banquet after that, but it ended before long. Lorraine's illusion magic was incredible, and the barrage of questions I got from the villagers afterward was exhausting. It was like that illusion made them think I was inhuman. Which I was, but still. After the second viewing, I could say with certainty that her depiction of my battle with the tarasque was a work of art, but it was hard to get past how exaggerated it was. Riri said she wanted to get that strong so she'd be my equal, but if she ever actually succeeded at matching that illusion, she'd be far beyond me. I hoped she wouldn't try to go too far.

"I guess not a lot of work's been done here," Lorraine said as we walked around the western edge of the village the next day.

The area was almost like a forest. There was no path to tread, as the one that had once been there was covered in weeds. It was highly likely that animals or monsters would approach, so the houses in the area had been abandoned long ago and left to rot. It was technically outside of the village, but sometimes children would come here to prove their courage, so it was often considered part of Hathara. It was a fairly open area, though, so if the weeds were picked, it would be livable enough.

"It's been like this since I was a kid. I heard that a long time ago, a monster came out of these woods and attacked some villagers. That's when they completely abandoned the area."

That was long before I was born, supposedly around when Gharb was young. She and the village elders were the only ones left with knowledge of that era.

"So you could stray just a little from the center and run into monsters? This is some terrifying territory."

"It's a small village. That's how it is."

Lorraine could only ask that because she came from the city. Monsters almost never appeared there. Hathara was especially rural, but most villages were constantly under threat. Cities had great walls and trained guards at their gates, but this was a different environment.

You might suggest that we all just move to the city, but that would be impossible for a number of reasons. For one, we would need homes, and the cost of rent in cities was nothing to scoff at. Anyone who sincerely planned to live in a city would need a job that paid a decent wage, but few local jobs would hire someone with a villager's education. That was the main issue keeping villagers from moving there. If they were willing to do anything, then they typically became adventurers, but this was a tough decision that quickly killed anyone without combat experience. Not everyone had mana or spirit either, so most villagers had next to no opportunities to move to a city. Others preferred not to leave their homeland, or they created products with materials only available in the area, or they had to stay because they worked at a nearby labor site, or any number of other reasons. Villages were dangerous, but living elsewhere wasn't always an option.

"I think it was behind this house," I said as I stopped in front of one of the dilapidated buildings. It looked familiar.

Lorraine looked up at it. "Looks just like all the others."

"Well, sure. What, did you think there'd be something special about it?"

"It has a shrine dedicated to some divine entity behind it, so I thought the house might serve a special purpose. It seems I thought wrong."

"I see what you're saying, but if that were true, it would've stuck in my memory more. Wait, it's probably that one."

There was a period of time when I would frequent this place, but years had passed since then. I seldom came to see it during my visits to the village either. As such, there was no path, so we had to push through the abundant plants to proceed.

"Here we are. It's surprisingly beautiful," I said when I found it.

"If this is beautiful to you, Rentt, then I don't know what's going on in your head," Lorraine said, eyeing me dubiously.

I could see why she would say that. The shrine hadn't fallen apart, but it had been damaged by storms, soiled by bird droppings, and overtaken by thick vines. Calling it beautiful was a stretch. Still, that didn't stop me.

"It's far more beautiful than when I first found it, if only because it's all put together."

"Was it in that bad of shape?"

"Yeah. The roof had completely rotted. Even the foundation was so eroded that some parts of it were as thin as a string. Just touching the shrine the wrong way could have made it collapse."

"And you went out of your way to fix it up anyway? You're so peculiar sometimes."

Lorraine looked baffled that I would put up with all that work. Thinking back on it, I was impressed with myself too.

"Anyway, I couldn't repair the building without knowing what it was supposed to look like in the first place, so I started by carefully taking the whole thing apart. I replaced the pieces that seemed like they wouldn't work anymore, which was most of them, so it's more or less a whole new building now. But there were at least a few parts in good shape, and the pillars looked like they would last a little longer. Somehow it came together decently in the end."

"So you spent all that time on this shrine, then left it untouched for a decade, and this is the result. Well, compared to the average building that hasn't been maintained in years, I suppose it is beautiful."

"Pretty much. Now, Lorraine, let's clean the place up." Lorraine cocked her head at me as I took a bucket, rags, and other cleaning supplies out of my magic bag. "Use magic to fill this bucket with water. I'll go cut the vines. We just need to finish this up by nightfall."

I'd very forcefully dragged her into it, but after Lorraine took another look at the shrine, she seemed to understand. "Well, you're only alive right now thanks to power granted to you by whatever lives here. As your friend, maybe I should express my thanks to them too," she said with a sigh as she picked up the bucket.

"Now that I see it fixed up, it's rather stunning," Lorraine said with satisfaction. Her face was messy with soot, but her expression looked bright under the setting sun. I knew how she felt. It took a long time, but if we managed to make this building more beautiful, then it was all worth it.

I was in a similar state, but my mask and robes blocked the filth, so I was surprisingly not that dirty. The mysterious robes I had gotten in that dungeon were of unbelievably high quality. Not only did they resist fire and poison, but they also seemed to resist dirt.

After that, Lorraine used magic to clean herself up. Moments later, she looked just as she had before we started.

"If you had just cast Linpio on the shrine too, this would have been a breeze," I said bluntly.

"What would have been the point?" she replied. "You wanted to clean it to show your gratitude. That means getting your own hands dirty, as with shrines of any religion. Besides, Linpio isn't as useful as it might seem. It won't help with grime that's stuck on too hard."

Lorraine demonstrated by casting Linpio on a random stick. The darkened parts remained the same, so it looked no more clean than if it had been washed with water. It was like how dust, blood, and ink would come off of skin, but blemishes wouldn't, much to the chagrin of maidens everywhere. It couldn't remove scabs either, actually. Ink also only came off if it hadn't fully dried yet.

Magic seemed convenient, but it wasn't. We still could have used it to eliminate surface-level filth, but the biggest reason not to do that was what Lorraine had pointed out. If we wanted to express our thanks, it was better to clean with our own hands. Even followers of the Church of the Eastern Sky, though some were magicians, cleaned their altars by hand at the end of each season. Linpio happened to be a life spell that even I could use, and it would have been faster and easier to use magic. But as a general rule, offering your appreciation required some toil on your part.

"Still, it was worth the effort. You can hardly tell this is the same shrine," I said as I looked at it again. All the filth was scrubbed off and all the vines cut away.

All this cleaning and repairing would go to waste if it just built up again while I was away, so we picked the weeds in the surrounding area too. All we left were the saplings because they seemed to grow away from the shrine. I didn't know what this shrine worshiped, but considering the nature of my divinity, it was presumably a plant-type divine spirit. If so, I didn't want to remove too many of the plants. But as far as the ones all over the shrine, I had to do away with them for the sake of human convenience. I felt a bit bad about it, but there was no better choice.

"Now that I see the full shrine, it looks like you did a fine job. You really are talented, Rentt," Lorraine said.

To say I agreed would be a bit prideful of me, but it was clearly better maintenance work than the average hobbyist could provide. I had trained under a professional, so of course that should go without saying. I wouldn't say I was top rate, but my craftsmanship would match an apprentice.

"I learned a lot in the village, so thank them. You never know what skills might come in handy. Now, shall we pray?"

That was the main reason we'd come here in the first place—to express our gratitude to whatever had blessed me. As for figuring out what that was, maybe asking the village elders or searching through old texts would shed some light on it. I didn't expect much, but it would be a nice thing to try.

First, I kneeled before the shrine and clasped my hands together. Lorraine followed suit. She didn't have to, but I guess she was playing along. Perhaps today convinced her to convert to whatever religion this shrine would fall under. A divine spirit with no followers probably didn't qualify for its own religion, but maybe that was rude to say.

Not long after we began to pray, I thought I heard a voice. "Lorraine, did you hear something?" I asked, confused.

Lorraine looked up and cocked her head. "No, nothing."

Assuming I'd imagined it, I began to pray again. "Thank you so much for granting me power all this time. Honestly, I don't have a lot of faith, but you're still watching over me for some reason. Without this power, I wouldn't be here right now. If you don't mind me asking, please continue to bless me going forward." That was the gist of my prayer.

In some corner of my mind, I also hoped I would find out what this divine spirit was. But such a demand would be uncouth, so I decided to keep it to myself. If I ever were to ask that, it would be better left for after I researched it in the village. Besides, divine spirits were supposed to be fickle in general, so even if I did ask, there was no telling if I would get an answer. That it blessed me at all was an unpredictable outcome.

"Unpredictable? You repaired my shrine. Blessing you is what any divine spirit would do, I'd think," said a dismayed voice.

This time it definitely wasn't my imagination. I looked around, but nobody else was here besides Lorraine.

"Rentt, I heard it too," Lorraine said. "Does somebody live around here?"

I shook my head. "No, the only houses here are the abandoned ones you saw. Sometimes kids explore the area, but it's otherwise deserted. If this village were closer to Maalt, I might think that thieves used these houses as hiding places, but there'd be no value in doing that in Hathara."

The village was far too removed from civilization. There was no use hiding from humans if it meant being attacked by monsters instead. Also, the people of Hathara were perceptive; any thieves who tried to hide here would be quickly found out.

"Then just who could have said that?" Lorraine muttered.

I looked at her stomach with shock. "Hey, Lorraine..."

"What?"

"Something's crawling under your clothes. What the heck is it?"

"My clothes?"

Only now did Lorraine look down and notice the squirming.

"What is it?" I wondered. "Are you doing some experiment where you carry a weird creature under your clothes?"

Lorraine thought for a bit. "No, not at the moment," she replied. That seemed to imply there were moments when she did let strange organisms live on her. As much as I wanted to ask about that, it wasn't the most pertinent subject.

"Anyway, can you take it out?"

"Oh, yes, let's see here," she said and jammed a hand under her clothes. She grabbed at something and then pulled it out.

"Didn't you take that thing from me before?" I asked.

"I believe so. What in the world is happening, though? It's moving by itself."

It was the figure of Lorraine that I'd carved from shrub ent wood. It was somehow moving on its own. Honestly, it was frightening.

"Could it be cursed?" I asked.

"No, I don't think so. I don't sense any of the evil presence that cursed objects exude. Although, I don't sense anything from your mask either," Lorraine said, the figure wriggling all the while. The way it moved seemed a bit lacking. I had given it limbs, so it could have at least tried to act more human. As its creator, I was disappointed.

"Are you the one who talked?" I asked the doll.

If I were to take a step back, this would look like a highly dangerous situation. Not in the sense that I was interacting with an unknown being without taking any precautions, mind you, but because I was seriously talking to a doll. There were dolls that could move on their own to some extent after being provided mana. They were used by puppet masters for shows or for adventuring. A talking doll wasn't that inconceivable, but society didn't look kindly upon puppet masters. They were believed to be a strange bunch, and that belief was correct. Becoming a puppet master required both a comprehension of advanced magic technology and an unparalleled passion for dolls, so they were often a little deranged. Some of them were normal, of course, but the oddballs were the ones who stood out.

I'd never even thought to dabble in puppet mastery, but if I wanted to, it would take some courage.

The figure turned to face me. "Yes, yes I did. Hello," it said, but its voice didn't match the movements of its mouth. What it said wasn't especially strange, but that made me uneasy. Lorraine and I exchanged a look before we continued the conversation.

"So, what are you, exactly?" I asked. "Based on where we are, I'm guessing you're the thing this shrine is dedicated to. Am I right?"

The doll abruptly got up. "That's mostly right," it said. "I'm only a fraction of my true self, though. My main shrine is elsewhere, and that's where you would find my main body, so I don't have much power here. I did bless you, but sorry it's such a lousy blessing. I only have two followers, so you can't expect too much."

There was so much to ask that I didn't know where to begin.

Lorraine pondered for a moment before asking, "First of all, are we right to assume you're a divine spirit?" That was a good place to start.

"I guess that's not technically wrong, but like I said, I'm a fraction of the divine spirit. I'm closer to just any old spirit. I've been away from my true self for so long that I'm on my own at this point."

"Who is your 'true self'?"

"Viroget, the God of Plants."

Viroget was a god with dominion over plants and fertility as well as war and harvests. He was a relatively dangerous god who would wage war for the sake of prosperity. He was said to be ruthless. The spirit in this figure, however, seemed pretty docile.

"Why did you inhabit this figure?" Lorraine asked.

"Well, without an object to dwell in, it's hard to materialize vividly enough for ordinary humans to see. That might be different with a proper temple, but this little shrine in the mountains isn't cutting it. I wanted to talk to you two and needed to find a way, and this figure happened to be perfect."

"What makes it perfect?"

"This was made from materials containing mana, right? By one of my followers, no less. We can't inhabit objects made from normal materials, so I happened to get lucky."

Lorraine happened to have been carrying this figure around, so this spirit got to meet us. It was certainly lucky, but I had to question why Lorraine still kept this on her in the first place. I decided to ask her about it later.

"Oh right, you said you have two followers. Who are they?" I asked.

The figure pointed to us. "Followers," it said.

Now, it wasn't as if I placed much faith in any gods. I did pray, but no more than a few times in the last decade. To call me a follower of this spirit seemed questionable.

The figure seemed to know what I was thinking. "Nobody else comes to this shrine, so it's you or nobody. I know the place has been abandoned. Wait, more importantly, I need to bless my new follower!" it suddenly shouted and then floated in the air. It shined and hovered in a circle around Lorraine, chanting some words I couldn't hear. Lorraine began to glow with a light I recognized.

"It's divinity."

"Divinity? This is?" Lorraine asked. She stared with shock at the light she gave off. She didn't look like a follower shaking with joy over being blessed by their god. Rather, she came across like a mad scientist delighted to find something new to study. There was no faith to be found in her, so I had to wonder if this spirit made the right choice. It did seem satisfied, however.

"Oh boy, a new follower. This calls for a celebration. Bring out the alcohol!" it said.

I wanted to ask if it was mistaking its shrine for a bar, but we did happen to have alcohol. Lorraine had wanted some of Hathara's strongest drinks for home, so she had taken the leftovers from last night. She had about twenty big bottles, so surely she could live with giving up one of them. She had received a number of bottles after showing her illusion magic at the banquet, but she had used my likeness for it. After embarrassing me like that, I deserved at least one.

When I took out one of the bottles, Lorraine looked at it somewhat wantingly, but she didn't complain. I took that to mean she accepted, so I presented it to the figure.

"Oh, I was kidding. You actually have some on you! You're the best follower I could ask for," the figure said and turned its wooden body toward me. I wondered how it would be able to drink anything, but my question was answered when the bottle began to float toward the figure. The cap remained on, but the liquid within vanished before my eyes.

"Wow, that's the stuff!" the figure said when it finished, acting no different than it had a minute ago. Maybe divine spirits didn't get drunk. If so, alcohol didn't seem like it would be much fun for them, unless they enjoyed it in ways that humans couldn't comprehend. I had no idea, but at least it was happy.

Meanwhile, Lorraine was trying out her newfound divinity. "This feels pretty different from magic. Rentt, I'm amazed you can switch between them so fluidly."

Mana and divinity were certainly different, as was spirit. Using more than one of them one after another was surprisingly difficult, but it was possible once you got used to it. I didn't have much power to work with, but I had a decade to test that power out, and I needed to make the best of what I had just to survive at all. When it came to control over energy, Lorraine wasn't going to outmatch me easily. As far as the strength and handling of spells, though, I couldn't beat her. I might have had an easier time switching, but that said nothing of the strength of her divinity itself.

"I've used all my powers to death already. I'm used to it. So how much divinity do you have?" I asked. "If it's more than me, I think I might cry."

"I only just obtained this power, so it's hard to say. I think it's a very small amount. I've only used a tiny bit, but it feels like I've already run dry," she answered.

I looked at Lorraine, and her divinity did seem to mostly be gone. She must have already used it up. If releasing a small amount was enough to run out, then she might have had a similar quantity to what I used to have.

"I told you it was a lousy blessing. This is the best a spirit like me can do. It was the same for Rentt. Wait, actually, I just noticed Rentt has a crazy amount of divinity. Why's that? It's around a hundred times more than what I gave you."

My divinity was a good deal greater than it used to be, but I thought that was thanks to something this spirit did. Apparently that wasn't the case. Now I was curious.

"So you didn't give me more divinity?" I asked. "I thought the strength and quantity of one's divinity was determined by its origins. I figured you were helping me through all the challenges I've had lately by strengthening your blessing or something." A god would try to protect their followers, so that made sense to me.

But the figure shook its head. "I'm not that nice. Or so I'd say, but with only two followers, I'd love to help you stay out of danger. But I'm extremely weak, you see. I can't even check on Rentt that often. Even talking to you like this right now requires a lot of effort."

"Then why did my divinity increase?" I asked.

The figure cocked its head and stared at me. "Well, it can be gradually increased if you work hard enough, but what happened to you isn't normal. It's probably got something to do with that weird mask. I sense a god, but I don't know which one."

"This?" It was the cursed mask Rina had bought me at the market. Aside from being irremovable, I never thought it had any effects. If what the spirit said was true, then this mask wasn't even cursed in the first place. It mentioned a god, but I didn't sense anything. Neither did Lorraine.

"It could be a holy item," the figure said. "That would explain why it's enhancing my blessing. Maybe you got a bit of an additional blessing from the mask's creator."

For the most part, humans had no way of knowing which gods blessed them. Your only hope was to infer, as I did when I gained divinity after repairing the shrine. This meant that my unthinkable increase in divinity came from another blessing I wasn't aware of, and it originated from this mask.

"Which god is it, exactly?"

"Who knows? Like I said, I don't know. If you really want to find out, why not go to the God of Appraisal's main temple? If you bring a holy item, the god himself might look at it for you."

Just then, the figure suddenly began to panic. Lorraine and I gave it strange looks.

"Looks like my time is up," it said, now speaking rapidly. "Next time you create something for me to inhabit, use better materials. Humanoid objects are the easiest to possess. I should be able to possess it no matter where you are, as long as you call for me."

"Wait! At least tell me your name," I shouted.

"My name? Nobody's given me a name. I'm part of Viroget, so call me Viro or Get or something. See you later!" it said lightly and then spewed what appeared to be steam.

For a brief moment, I thought I saw the silhouette of someone in the steam, but then it disappeared into the air. The wooden figure blackened and crumbled into sand within seconds.

"What? Can you do something about this, Rentt?!" Lorraine cried. She was distraught for some reason, but there was nothing I could do.

"It's just a figure. What's the big deal?" I asked. It wasn't as if Viro or Get or whichever name I wanted to settle on had died. It was just something I'd made.

"It's a huge deal! Oh no, it's completely fallen apart."

By the time the silky sand fell to the ground, Lorraine gave up and slumped over.

"Did you like it?" I asked. "I could make a million of those for you. That divine spirit asked us to make it another vessel anyway."

Lorraine's face brightened a bit. "Right, I suppose that's fine. So the figure acted as a vessel for it, then?" she asked seriously.

"That's what it seemed like. But it said it can only possess something that contains mana, so we'll have to consider which materials to use. After it's made, we can supposedly ask the spirit to come possess it at any time."

I didn't know whether it would actually work, but it was worth a try. There was more I wanted to ask the spirit. It said the location didn't matter, so it didn't even have to be in Hathara. It was said that the gods dwelled everywhere and nowhere. By that, they meant that as long as you had faith, it didn't matter where you were. But shrines and temples were like doors that connected our world to theirs, making it easy for them to interact with us, from what I had heard. This was a subject best left to religious folk, though. I could ask one of them for more details. I didn't know whether to consider myself lucky, but I did happen to know a few clergy members. Lillian and Myullias and even Nive might have counted. Albeit, she wasn't part of the church, and it seemed more like she was using them than anything. She might know about gods and spirits, though, so maybe she would be just as good to ask. I didn't especially want to rely on her, however.

"It's odd how the spirit is letting us name it. If it's supposed to be part of Viroget, I wouldn't have expected it to be so casual," Lorraine said.

Viroget was the God of Plants, but if this spirit was a piece of him, then it didn't seem unreasonable to go ask him for a name. But maybe this was just how gods were. This was my first contact with such a being and I couldn't judge all of them by this experience alone, but I wouldn't describe this entity as especially holy. It had said it was more of a normal spirit than a divine one, so maybe I only thought this because it didn't turn out to be an important god. Or maybe all gods were this carefree. I hoped not.

"I thought it was awfully casual too. Do you think all gods are like this?" I asked.

She pondered the question for a moment. "It's said that gods are so imposing that they're hard to defy, that they carry themselves with an air of divine majesty, and that they're far outside our reach. But that spirit was nothing like that. Not to be rude or anything."

Lorraine had no faith in any particular religion, but she seemed to have some reverence toward gods. She chose her words carefully, but it amounted to her saying that this spirit was not at all godlike. I felt the same way.

"I'd bet the spirit would say the same thing. Anyway, I'll make another figure some time. It'll be best to carve it from something with more mana. It sounded like possessing a vessel and staying in it demands some degree of effort." I wouldn't want to use the same materials again just so it could leave after a few minutes. I would either have to find higher quality materials in a dungeon or buy them somewhere.

"We can save that for when we return to Maalt, I suppose. At least this trip wasn't a waste of time. We learned more about your mask, and we learned that we could ask the God of Appraisal to look at it."

"I find that a bit sketchy. Hopefully we don't just go to that temple, get no information from their appraisers, and leave empty-handed."

The God of Appraisal had dominion over the worth and evaluation of items, and he was primarily worshiped by merchants and nobles. All priests for the God of Appraisal were capable appraisers, so they always had visitors coming to determine the value of their possessions. I had never been there myself, but it sounded like the ideal place to learn about my mask.

There was a problem, however. The priests had a strict attitude about cursed items. You could bring one to be appraised, but if they found out it was cursed, they would insist on purifying it. If you had the misfortune of being interested in owning cursed items, you never wanted to take them there. That included myself, so I thought I could never go. But if the spirit was correct, then my mask was actually holy. In that case, I could go get it appraised without any issues. The worst that could happen is they purified it and it fell off, which wouldn't be so bad.

If there was any problem, it was that my true nature might be discovered, but the appraisers at the temple simply used immense knowledge and experience to do their job. They had no special ability to determine the nature of something on sight, so they wouldn't be able to see that I was a vampire. It would be no more dangerous than when I went out to town.

We decided to leave this for after we returned to Maalt. The goal would be to go to the God of Appraisal's temple. The problem was that we were told to go to the main temple. There was a branch temple in Yaaran, but that supposedly wasn't good enough. I had some idea as to why. Temples and shrines were close to the world of gods and spirits, with the main temples being the easiest places for them to enter our world. But historically there were virtually no instances of gods coming to our world, Viro aside. Viro had shown himself to us pretty casually, so maybe the rules around that were surprisingly loose. He said it took some effort, so maybe it was just his tone that was casual and he actually arrived under very strict circumstances. I imagined it was something like that and the God of Appraisal could only come to his main temple. Viro was closer to a normal spirit, or something of a minor god, but the God of Appraisal was quite significant and had been worshiped since ancient times. Humans of high status were similarly impossible to meet with before overcoming some barriers. You needed the right place, the right time, the right number of people, and more. If it was the same for gods, then I could understand why I'd have to go to their main temple.

However, that temple was in another country. We would be forced to leave on a journey. As long as I still had to teach Alize and collect Dragon Blood Blossoms for Laura, that would pose a problem. But that was something to discuss when we got back.

"Well, anyway, that takes care of business here," Lorraine said. "All that remains is to go visit your teacher. The sun has set, though. Should we?"

She must have meant Gharb. I had forgotten that she invited us. I didn't know if she had something in particular to tell us or if she just wanted to chat after all these years apart. She was the most mysterious of the villagers, so I couldn't begin to guess what she was thinking. She might have had reasons that I wasn't even considering.

That was somewhat of a scary thought, but ignoring her invitation wasn't an option. She was one of the people who formed the foundation of my adventuring skills, after all. Disciples had to be loyal to their teachers.

The time of day was a problem, though. The sun had gone down. She might have expected us to show up in the afternoon. There were no magic lamps like we had in Maalt, so it was very much nighttime. Everyone returned home to have dinner and then went straight to bed so they could wake up as the sun rose the next morning. Their way of life was nothing like in the city. In Maalt terms, visiting someone now would be like visiting them after midnight, a little bit insensible.

I was hesitant, but that didn't stop me. "We should go. If she tells us to come back tomorrow, we can do that instead."

So we decided to head to Gharb's house.

Chapter 4: The Secret of Hathara

"Oh, you're finally here. Do you know how long I've been waiting?"

As soon as we got to Gharb's house and knocked on the door, it opened to reveal the mischievous old woman on the other side. She had always looked scary to me, and even now I couldn't think differently. On some instinctive level, I couldn't disobey her when I saw that face. That wasn't to say she looked like a monster or anything. Besides, I had been far more fearsome when I was a ghoul.

"Come now, don't just stand there. Come in. I have another guest waiting inside," Gharb continued.

I couldn't have guessed who the other guest was. Hathara was small enough that all the villagers treated each other like relatives. Coming over to another house for dinner was a common occurrence, so for most this was nothing unusual. However, Gharb didn't often have guests, so I began to suspect something.

We went inside and followed Gharb until we came to a room with a dinner table. There was already a man seated there, and he raised his hand in greeting. "Hey, Rentt, there you are. And you're the lady with the illusion magic?"

I recognized him, of course. He had been at the banquet as well. His name was Capitan, and he was the head of the village hunters. He was also another one of my teachers. He had taught me how to handle hunting knives and bows, how to properly traverse a forest, and how to survive in the wilderness.

Capitan had two teenage children and was getting along in years, but his skills had yet to diminish. Muscles covered his body like armor, impressive enough to match any swordsman in Maalt. But even without that, he could more than likely best them thanks to his mastery over spirit.

Spirit was a skill that all adventurers should have, but not all of them did. Capitan, however, could utilize it at an advanced level. All of the hunters he led knew how to use spirit, and while they weren't as adept as him, they were decent enough. I was probably strong enough at this point that I could beat those hunters, but I didn't know if I could beat Capitan. I'd never once seen him put up a serious fight; he didn't need to. This wasn't the type of man who should be languishing into obscurity in this mountain village, but he seemed content anyway. Maybe he wasn't that ambitious, but he was a difficult man to understand. He was strange, in any case.

Lorraine had already met him at the banquet last night. She told me he'd asked a lot of questions about how I fought in the illusion she presented. Just knowing that made me feel uncomfortable. In fact, this whole situation was uncomfortable. Two of my teachers were here—three if you counted Lorraine as my magic teacher.

"Why are you here, Capitan?" I asked and cocked my head.

While I referred to Gharb as Teacher, I simply called Capitan by his first name. A long time ago, back when he was teaching me all these skills, I had called him Teacher and he'd said that was a poor fit for him. Maybe he really thought that to some extent, but sometimes it seemed like he was just being shy. Sometimes I'd called him Teacher anyway. It cheered him up, which then made him unspeakably mad. But he was generally a gentle person.

I still didn't know why he was here, though. It was bizarre.

"Just wanted to see how much you've grown," Capitan said. "I've been talking with Gharb about you. And that illusion lady there, Lorraine, showed us how you fight too."

Lorraine had exaggerated her illusion in more ways than one, but she had faithfully recreated the way I fought, at least. She'd even included some minor details. I was a bit stunned by it, but at the same time, I got to see where I could improve, so it was worth the watch. But I didn't know how to feel about my teachers watching it.

"Capitan, don't scare him," Gharb chided. "Rentt, we're not here to criticize you; don't worry about that. We just have some questions."

I tried to figure out what they might want to ask, but there were too many possibilities to list. I looked to Lorraine as I decided what to say. I didn't know if I'd be able to hide anything from these two in the first place.

"But not just yet," Gharb continued. "It would be rude to make you do all the talking, so we decided to tell you two about the secret of this village. We told Ingo that we would, of course."

"What secret? Not to insult Hathara, but I thought it was just a small village in the mountains. You and Capitan, though, have skills the likes of which I've hardly even seen in Maalt."

I had thought it odd that so many such people were in a rural village, but it wasn't impossible. There were more stories than I could count of Platinum-class adventurers who suddenly retired one day and returned to the village they grew up in. A fair number of similar tales about military generals and court magicians existed too. You could go to almost any destitute village and find an incredibly distinguished person walking around in ordinary clothes. Because of that, I'd always assumed there was nothing so strange about Hathara. But the way Gharb talked, it sounded like there was some greater reason behind it all.

I looked at Lorraine, and she stared back with an expression that said she knew something was weird about this place all along. She had thought something was off the whole time we'd been here.

"Yes, you're correct for the most part," Gharb replied. "Correct with regards to most of the villagers, rather. You never thought this was any more than an ordinary village, did you? Well, maybe you thought it was just a bit out of the ordinary, but nothing more than that, I'm sure."

"I did think you and Capitan seemed out of place, but that was about it." Their talent was great enough that they'd be highly sought after in Maalt too. Gharb would be valued as a doctor, while Capitan would be valued as a warrior. And yet they stayed here. I often thought about this during my adventures in Maalt.

"So from the sound of it, this really isn't a regular village?" Lorraine asked.

Capitan answered, "No, you can say it's a regular village now. Like the old lady said, that's what it is to most of the villagers. That's how it's always been, and that's how it'll always be. But to me, Gharb, and Ingo, it's a bit different."

The three people Capitan listed were effectively in charge of the village. Such a small population didn't need a council or proper governmental roles like Maalt did. These three were the ones to consult if there was a problem, and as far as the villagers were concerned, they were the ones who made the decisions. Ingo was included because he was the mayor, of course; Gharb was viewed as the most knowledgeable person in the village; and Capitan was the leader of the strongest group of fighters.

And to these three, this was no ordinary village. I wondered what that was supposed to mean. So did Lorraine, naturally. I didn't expect it to have anything to do with why I became undead, but maybe it would explain why that shrine was treated the way it was.

I'd lived most of my life in this village, and the idea that it had a secret tickled my curiosity.

Both Lorraine and I were curious by nature. If we weren't, we wouldn't be adventurers. An adventurer was someone who'd do anything, including risking their own life, to learn even one of the world's secrets. Now that we knew this village had one, leaving before hearing the rest of the story wasn't an option.

"So, what is Hathara to the three of you?" I asked, getting straight to the heart of the matter.

"I could tell you here and now, but you wouldn't really get a feel for what I'm talking about," Gharb said. "I'd like to talk about this more tomorrow. There's a place I'd like the four of us to go. That's why I told you to come over after you'd looked at the shrine, but now it's gotten dark. It'd be dangerous to go at this time of night. Tonight, you can just have dinner here. Come over again tomorrow morning, and I'll tell you everything."

The old woman smiled.

"What in the world does she know? I can't wait to find out," Lorraine said, enjoying herself.

It was now the next morning, and we were on the way to Gharb's house. I felt much the same as her. Seemingly ordinary villages that hid a special secret had been the topic of stories for ages. Only a select few were lucky enough to go on adventures like that, while average adventurers like us would go through life without encountering anything so exciting. But now it was happening, on this visit back to my hometown no less. There was no reason not to be excited.

"Neither can I," I said, "but I'm impressed they were able to hide it all this time. And not just from me but from the whole village."

This secret was known only to Gharb, Capitan, and Ingo, according to them. If it was such a major secret, then I had to respect them for being able to keep it for so long. Maybe I hadn't noticed because I left when I was young and it had been a while, but Riri and Fahri spent almost all of their time here, and they still didn't know. It was just amazing. Either that or the secret wasn't that big a deal. That wouldn't be much fun, though, so I hoped it was.

"They managed to hide it, yes, but they made it sound like it wasn't something especially relevant to the villagers in the modern day regardless. It may be no more than they've never needed to bring it up," Lorraine guessed, though neither of us knew whether she was correct just yet.

I looked straight ahead and saw Gharb's house. "Oh, we're here. Hey!" I shouted.

Waiting at the door, the old woman and the robust man gazed at us. Gharb was wearing a coat she only put on for long outings, and Capitan was in his hunting gear. They were both clearly ready to go somewhere. Capitan even had a hunting knife at his hip, a bow across his shoulders, and a quiver on his back. But we were also equipped heavily enough to travel outside the village. I'd worn lighter clothing for most of my visit, but now I was in adventuring gear. I had my sword with me, and Lorraine had her wand and dagger.

"All right, everyone's here," Gharb said, looking at my outfit. "That looks good on you, Rentt. You've grown to look the part of an adventurer."

She meant the robe, the mask, and the sword, all things that made me look suspicious. I had told Gharb about how I couldn't take the mask off, but everyone else jumped to the conclusion that this was the fashion in Maalt. I prayed to Viro that if they ever went to Maalt to go sightseeing, they wouldn't all walk around wearing masks. Then I thought I heard someone say that was a silly prayer and not what praying was for, but maybe it was my imagination.

"I'm not choosing to look like this," I answered. "The robe is surprisingly comfortable and convenient, though, so I treasure it."

"Convenient how?" Capitan asked.

I couldn't ignore a question from one of my teachers. I didn't always answer honestly, but I couldn't not respond.

"It's stronger than your average metal armor, and it deflects poison. It doesn't get dirty either," I said, starting to wonder how much it would be worth if I sold it. It was hard to imagine life without it now, so I wouldn't do that, but it was an interesting question. If I met the God of Appraisal, maybe I could ask him to appraise the robe too.

"Huh, mind if I shoot an arrow at it?" Capitan asked with amusement.

I quickly shook my head. "Yes, I'd definitely mind that! You might actually be able to pierce through it!"

I didn't just say that to flatter him. When he was serious about firing an arrow, it always pierced its target. The bow itself wasn't especially strong, so he had the power of spirit to thank for that. Charging swords, spears, and other handheld weapons with spirit required a fair amount of training, but it was an achievable goal. Doing the same with a weapon that left contact with the body, however, was exceedingly difficult. But Capitan could do it. His arrows could even break boulders. Even with my robe, there was no guarantee I'd survive. It would probably be fine, but it wasn't worth the risk.

Capitan looked disappointed by my refusal. "Oh well. Either way, let's do a little sparring later. I want to see what you've got."

This conversation was taking a turn for the worse. I honestly didn't want to have to deal with that. Capitan was one of the people who had taught me to fight, after all. I'd learned most of my swordsmanship from the adventurer who came to the village, but I had learned my footwork and such from Capitan. My newfound physical abilities were probably enough for me to win, but I couldn't say for sure. I'd never seen Capitan when he got serious.

In any case, I couldn't refuse to spar. A pupil has to obey their master. "Fine," I said with a sigh. "Later. So where are we going?"

"The northern forest," Gharb answered. "To its deepest depths."

I was a bit shocked. Nobody was supposed to enter the northern forest. It was teeming with monsters so powerful that even Hathara's hunters steered clear.

"Is that why you're both fully equipped?" I asked.

It made sense. I'd never seen Gharb fight before, but she was probably a top-rate magician, according to Lorraine. Capitan was also a top-rate warrior, in my opinion. They'd be more readily able to enter a forest that was off-limits to the villagers of Hathara. But for some reason, they seemed a bit tense today. It was just that dangerous, presumably.

"Well, yes," Gharb said. "Stay alert, you two. This is no ordinary forest. Now let's go."

Gharb led the way, so we began to follow behind her.

Capitan chopped a goblin's head clean off with his hunting knife. Three other goblins rushed at him with rusty daggers, trying to take him off guard, but he sidestepped and sliced through them all. Not far from him, Gharb was launching blades of wind at a giant spider monster called an akavish gadol, severing its legs. The spider tried to attack Gharb with its remaining legs, but she was nimble for her age and dodged every one of them. She was a magician and presumably knew physical enhancement techniques, so it wasn't that unusual, but seeing an old woman jumping around like a monkey was somewhat frightening. She did it all while unleashing spells, too. Most magicians fought more like stationary cannons, but Gharb was fundamentally different. She fought like a magic swordsman or a combat mage. Her punches seemed like they might actually be stronger than her magic, scarily enough.

"We're the adventurers here, and we didn't even get the chance to do our jobs," Lorraine muttered some time later, after the battle had ended. We were surrounded by monster corpses.

Ever since I was little, I was told to stay out of the northern forest, and it turned out to be every bit as threatening as it was built up to be. Few forests had so many monsters, except in the event of a surge or overflow. There were plenty of other territories that the world generally considered dangerous, and those might also be different if I were to enter them, but I never knew there was a place like this near my hometown.

"How does Hathara survive with all these monsters nearby?" I whispered.

Gharb heard me and said, "Not a problem. These monsters won't come to Hathara."

That was reassuring if true, but I didn't know what proof she had. I knew that most strong monsters had their own turf they never left, but there were also plenty of goblins, slimes, and other common low-level monsters here. It didn't make sense for them to only operate within a certain area. They survived on their reproductive abilities rather than their strength, so they always tried to aggressively expand to other locations. The idea of sticking to one place was foreign to them. Goblins did sometimes have their own settlements, but if they were hostile to humans, they'd try to conquer a human village and move in after it reached a certain size. Slimes were more simple than that. They just constantly multiplied and went everywhere. As such, I would think that their presence here meant they could easily find their way to Hathara.

But while Gharb and Capitan appeared to understand our questions, they just kept advancing deeper into the forest. They seemed to be implying that they would tell us when we got there. Lorraine and I looked at each other, shook our heads futilely, and continued to follow along.

"Here we are," Gharb said after some hours of walking around the forest, right around when I was starting to get fed up.

"Is this a fortress? It looks pretty old," Lorraine whispered.

It was indeed, by all appearances, some kind of fortress. It was like a small castle made of stone, but the years had not been kind to it. Some parts of it were in great disrepair. It was also overgrown with plants, covering almost its entire surface with greenery. If you were to gaze in this direction from Hathara, you'd think it was nothing but part of the forest. But there was certainly a fortress here.

I never knew there was anything like this near Hathara, so it came as a bit of a shock. "Do you think this is the secret of Hathara?" I asked.

"Probably so. I'm curious as to when it was built, but it doesn't look new, I can say that," Lorraine replied.

To be honest, we were disappointed that this just seemed to be some ancient ruin near the village. It was a reasonably significant secret from a historical perspective, but you could find ruins like these anywhere if you did a little searching. Some places even used their ancient ruins as tourist attractions. Considering that, I didn't think this secret was that impressive. Unless there was something special about these ruins.

Noticing our doubts, Gharb and Capitan walked further. "This way. Don't panic," they said.

It sounded like there was something else after all. I started to think that maybe I wouldn't be let down.

We entered the fortress. It looked as old inside as it did on the outside, the collapsed parts drawing the most attention. But it also looked like it had been cleaned up to some degree. There was enough floor space for people to walk around, which was a bit unnatural. My best guess was that Gharb and Capitan frequented this place and cleaned it up themselves. It wasn't entirely clear, but most of the villagers didn't come here, so that was the only possibility that came to mind.

We walked a while longer and arrived at a spacious area. "What is this place?" I asked.

"Most likely an audience room for a king, lord, or other prestigious person," Lorraine explained. "Perhaps in ancient times a powerful family lived in this region. Something like that."

In the back of the room was a raised section of the floor upon which sat a stone chair. Presumably it would have been covered in cloth in the past, but now the stone surface was exposed. All things faded with time. Whoever it was that once wielded power from this room, they weren't even remembered by history. Their role was now held by Gharb, Capitan, and Ingo, as the leaders of the village. However, I sensed no reverence for this room from either of the two who attended us.

"Over here. It's this room," they said and proceeded into a hallway next to the throne. This room apparently didn't matter.

We followed along, and when we reached our destination, we were shocked.

153

"It couldn't be. Why is this here?" Lorraine murmured, staring at the drawing covering the entire floor. It was an enormous magic circle that glowed with a pale blue light. I recognized this magic circle, and as a magician, Lorraine did as well. "It's a teleportation circle," she groaned.

Teleportation circles were almost exclusively found in dungeons, so naturally there was no reason for one to be here. Nobody would have known how to draw it. Well, perhaps that wasn't necessarily true. They could be copied by following a diagram. In fact, that was easy to do. But even if you copied it perfectly, the magic circle wouldn't activate. There was just something about how they worked that we didn't know. As such, new teleportation circles could only be found in dungeons. Some dungeons also changed their internal structure with each passing day, and in the depths of those dungeons, teleportation circles could be created or destroyed.

But there was no dungeon here. This building was likely a man-made fortress, so Lorraine and I had to wonder how a teleportation circle could be here.

Gharb and Capitan looked at our shocked faces with satisfied smiles.

"Looks like you're surprised," Gharb said. "After you came here dressed like that and with this girlfriend accompanying you, and after she used that illusion magic and all, you've been the ones surprising us for this entire visit. Now it feels like we've gotten back at you somehow, so that's nice."

Capitan nodded. "I was worried you might say this was nothing special in Maalt. We don't know what sort of magic research is going on in the big city, so they could have discovered how teleportation circles work by now."

There was a lot I could have commented on in those last two statements, but after thinking about it a bit, I settled on asking the most pertinent question. "Why is this here? No human could have made this, and they certainly aren't in any city in Yaaran. You wouldn't even find them in significantly larger cities."

By that, I was thinking of Lorraine's hometown. If the secrets of teleportation circles had been uncovered, Lorraine would know about it. Her shock could only mean that not even the Lelmudan Empire knew how to create them. The empire was centered around its military, however, and the military had classified information that a simple scholar like Lorraine wouldn't be privy to. But according to her, they would try to conquer the continent if they could, and teleportation circles would make it possible for them to send troops and supplies anywhere at any time. If they had that technology, Yaaran would have been destroyed long ago. Not that the Lelmudan Empire was the only advanced country in the world, but they were certainly among the most advanced, and not even their most cutting-edge research could explain teleportation circles.

"We can't make them either, mind you," Gharb answered slowly. "But this is here because the theory that humans can't create teleportation circles is partially wrong."

"What does that—" I started to ask, but Gharb cut me off.

"Well, just enter it and you'll figure it out. I'll go on ahead. Come, Capitan," she said and dragged him onto the teleportation circle with her. It began to glow, and the two of them gradually faded away until the last remaining light dissolved into the air, leaving only me and Lorraine.

We looked at each other.

"I know I say a lot of things are fascinating, but this is really fascinating, Rentt. What is with your village?" Lorraine said, more excited than usual. Her scholar's spirit must have been fired up.

I understood the feeling since I was pretty thrilled myself. This was absolutely nuts. I figured the village had some secrets, but this one was world-class. It was like something legendary adventurers would come across in an old story. My life of going to gloomy dungeons and trying desperately to vanquish a dozen boring monsters every day felt far behind me. Which it actually was, but I digress.

"I don't know, but I guess we should see where this takes us," I said, looking at the teleportation circle. I had used countless teleportation circles in dungeons, and I was sure that Lorraine had too. But seeing one outside of a dungeon was a first for me. Of course, it would be my first time using one outside a dungeon too, so that was scary in a number of ways. I had no idea where I'd end up or if I could even make it back here after. Gharb and Capitan hadn't thought twice about using it, so it was probably fine, but my instincts told me this was dangerous. My old habit of being overly cautious was showing itself. I felt like I'd been relatively bold as of late, but I was still a cowardly, low-ranking adventurer at heart.

Lorraine, however, felt differently. "If it were dangerous, they wouldn't have gone off without us like that. I'm sure nothing will happen. All right, Rentt, let's go," she said and yanked me by the arm onto the teleportation circle.

Personally, I still wanted time to mull it over, but it was too late now. She was right, though. Logically, there was no danger here. There was no reason there would be, but I was still a tiny bit scared. It was sort of like looking down from a tall cliff with a safety rope around your waist. You know you'll be safe, but it's still terrifying.

But now I was on it, so there was no going back. Lorraine, by contrast, looked eager to see what would happen. Then the magic circle generated a torrent of light, and we disappeared.

When I next opened my eyes, I heard Gharb teasing me. "Oh, there you are. I thought maybe you'd chickened out."

"I was scared the first time I got brought here too," Capitan said, chiding Gharb. "You're the only one who wouldn't be freaked out by this."

I looked around and was relieved to see them both unharmed. Lorraine was present and fine as well. The teleportation circle had apparently worked. Not that Gharb and Capitan would have had us use it if it didn't.

"But what in the world is this place?" Lorraine asked, looking around curiously. "It's dark. Are these walls? Is this some cave somewhere?"

I checked my surroundings too, and it did appear to be a cave. The glossy walls of stone were a bit moist. "Oh, but it's bright over there," I said when I stared off into the distance and saw some light, presumably shining in from the exit. Maybe the teleportation circle was hidden in a cave to make it hard to find. That would explain why it had never been discovered.

While we were thinking to ourselves, Gharb and Capitan looked at each other and grinned. "Well, we're almost to our destination," Gharb said. "Come along."

We still didn't know where we were going, but all we could do was follow them. At least we knew it wasn't dangerous.

"The way Gharb is leading us through this cave makes me feel like we're being guided to the afterlife," Lorraine joked as she looked at Gharb's back. From behind she looked kind of like the Grim Reaper, a denizen of the afterlife who invited the living to places unknown. Walking next to her, Capitan could have been a reaper knight, one of the Grim Reaper's minions. It was easy to see where Lorraine got that idea, especially when they wouldn't give us a single hint about where we were going. But they obviously didn't want us dead, so that wasn't worth worrying about. Hopefully.

I momentarily questioned my faith when we neared the light from the exit I saw earlier. I heard a gust of wind, and then something massive appeared before us.

"What?!" Lorraine yelled and grabbed her staff. Similarly, I drew my sword. But strangely, Gharb and Capitan did no such thing. In fact, they walked right up to the thing that approached us.

"There, there," Gharb said and reached out her hand to stroke its head.

I couldn't believe it. But however unbelievable it may have been, Gharb and Capitan reacted as if nothing was unusual. From the look of it, we were wrong to draw our weapons. We slowly put them away.

"Hey, Teacher, what is that?" I asked, inquiring of the creature Gharb was petting. It was far taller than a human, at least five meters in height, and its whole body was covered in black stripes. The creature looked just like a massive tiger. Its mouth was large enough to easily devour not only Gharb's head but her entire body. And yet it was playing with her like a cat. It seemed to enjoy the petting, and its eyes expressed loyalty to Gharb.

"Can't you see? It's a tiger."

"Are you kidding me?" I complained, unable to hide my frustration.

Gharb laughed. "Sorry, just joking around. Of course it's not just a tiger. This is a powerful monster called a shahor melechnamer. You'd know more about that than I do, I would think."

She meant that as adventurers, we should be more informed about monsters. I could immediately tell what type of monster it was when I saw it, so she was right about that. But that wasn't what I meant to ask. I wanted to know why it acted like Gharb's pet. Shahor melechnamers weren't something you could find in any old monster habitat, and a single one of them was strong enough to take on an entire army. Vanquishing one would be a job for a Platinum-class adventurer, at the very least, but ideally they would need to be Mithril-class. That's the level of monster we were looking at here. For Gharb to just go up and treat it like a typical cat, she deserved to be called crazy.

"It's not the type of monster that I'm confused about," I said. "Why isn't it attacking you? These aren't exactly common pets."

Monster tamers could tame many types of monsters, but they were generally ones that had a history of becoming friendly with humans. Not all monsters could be tamed. It was only once in every few centuries that someone would miraculously tame a powerful monster, and those people were showered in accolades. If Gharb was a monster tamer who tamed a shahor melechnamer, she would be considered legendary.

"It's not really me that it likes. It's my blood," Gharb said. "Come over here, Rentt."

I really, really didn't want to, but Gharb wouldn't listen. I stood stiffly in place until she dragged me up to the monster. I looked at it again now that I was up close. It was enormous. And horrifying. From its eyes I got the sense that it was intelligent, which made it all the more fearsome. This monster wasn't here for no reason. It had some objective. I just hoped it didn't want to gather us all in one place so it could eat us. But if that were what it wanted, it probably would have done so already.

To my surprise, the shahor melechnamer's attitude didn't change at all when it looked at me. Rather, it nuzzled against me with its head. Its fur felt nicer than I expected. It also purred. Monster or not, it was still a cat, I guess. But I still didn't know why it liked me so much when we had only just met. Gharb said it liked her blood, so I assumed that meant Hatharan blood. I was a vampire now, though. Maybe some of my Hatharan blood still flowed through my body regardless. In any case, the monster didn't seem to be a threat.

I didn't know how Lorraine would react though. Maybe she'd be unexpectedly frightened by this huge tiger, or maybe she'd observe it as calmly as ever. Curious, I looked behind me, and the look on Lorraine's face defied expectations. It was like a mix of confusion and astonishment, a reasonable response to this particular monster. But still, something was a bit strange. It didn't seem like she was reacting to seeing a powerful monster.

"Hey, Lorraine, what's wrong?" I asked. "You're acting weird."

"A shahor melechnamer, an ancient fortress, the teleportation circles, the cave... Oh, never mind, it couldn't be what I'm thinking," she muttered and shook her head. "Sorry, I kind of lost my cool. I'm just stunned by everything we've seen."

It sounded like she'd noticed some connection between all these things, but I didn't know what. I decided to ask her later.

"Teacher, Capitan! Can Lorraine get close to it too?" I asked from afar. Lorraine wasn't from Hathara, so I thought the monster might attack her.

"It won't hurt her as long as we're around," Gharb said. "And by we, I'm including you, Rentt. Nothing to worry about." She beckoned to Lorraine.

If I were her, I wouldn't have so readily believed that, but Lorraine had guts. She approached the shahor melechnamer and reached out her hand. The beast turned to look at Gharb for a moment. When the old woman nodded, the monster bowed its head to Lorraine. It even purred when she petted it. It seemed as long as a villager was present, this creature wouldn't harm any humans. I didn't know if it was commanded to behave this way or it was just in its nature, but that wasn't important for the time being.

"Is this the village secret? The fact that you have this pet?" I asked.

Gharb shook her head. "No, there's something else that more deserves to be called a secret. This just came here to greet us. Let's go," she said and walked off toward the exit to the cave.

We were almost to the exit now, at which point I was sure we'd see some outdoor scenery. But I was wrong.

"Is this a city?" I wondered aloud. My words echoed quietly.

What we saw appeared to be some sort of city, but there were no signs of human life anywhere. These were probably ruins, and particularly big ones at that. Several cities the size of Maalt could have occupied this space. There were buildings as far as the eye could see. But somehow we didn't seem to be on the surface, because for as vast as this place was, there was still a ceiling. The outer walls were made of stone like those of the cave we just came from, and the ceiling was likely the same.

I could see lights up there. They twinkled softly like stars in the sky. There were countless lights in the city as well, from what I could only guess were magic lamps, illuminating the whole area. It looked so grand that you wouldn't think the city was dead. If this place were discovered, it could easily become a popular destination for couples thanks to the romantic feel of it all. If this was the secret they were showing us, I couldn't really complain. The idea that a small village was hiding something so remarkable was awe-inspiring in more ways than one.

"What in the world is this place?" I asked.

"A city," Gharb answered.

"Oh, come on."

"Don't look at me like that; I'm kidding with you. It's true, though. This is a city. An ancient one destroyed long ago. I'm sure you've both heard of the Ancient Kingdom."

"Yes, of course." That name was famous among adventurers. It was a country that might have possessed the technology to make magic bags. It was a highly advanced and prosperous nation, and it was shrouded in mystery. We called it the Ancient Kingdom, but its real name was long forgotten. Remnants of its advanced technology existed throughout the world to be discovered once in a blue moon, indirectly proving that such a civilization must have existed, but that was all we knew. I didn't know what that had to do with this, though. I could guess, but I had no way to be sure everything Gharb said was true. I waited for her to elaborate.

Gharb paused before she spoke again. "This city was built by the descendants of the Ancient Kingdom. And the citizens of Hathara, including you, Rentt, are descended from them. That's the secret of the village," she said in a terribly casual manner.

This was a pretty shocking revelation, to say the least. I thought I just lived in one of a million villages, but it turned out my origins were the thing of legend. A lot of villages might claim something like this, but here we had explicit proof. Technology capable of creating a city this size underground wasn't exactly widely available. It could be done in the modern day with enough resources and manpower, but this had been built far in the past. Not only that, but they had made magic lamps that were still running to this day, which meant there was presumably some other functional technology leftover too.

I had plenty of questions, but Lorraine spoke before I could, delivering something even more surprising. "It was built by descendants from the Ancient Kingdom? Certainly not. This is Good King Felt's dungeon city, isn't it?!"

"Lorraine, what the hell are you talking about?" I asked, as the person least likely to understand what was going on. Neither Gharb nor Capitan seemed at all perturbed by what Lorraine said, so they must have known what she meant.

"I've told you about it before, haven't I? It's not a city with a dungeon around it but a city inside a dungeon," Lorraine answered, reminding me.

"Wasn't that in your homeland, though? Meaning it would be in the Lelmudan Empire?" After I said that, I remembered that we came here by teleportation circle. Then I got a vague idea as to what had happened.

Lorraine noticed that I'd figured it out and went on. "That's right. I've seen this all before. This underground dungeon with a ravishing ancient city, the monsters who attack all trespassers, and even their ruler, the shahor melechnamer. This is a dungeon in the Lelmudan Empire known as the Old Insect Dungeon. We're on the sixtieth floor, also known as Good King Felt's Dungeon City."

I was still at a complete loss, but it looked like I was the only one. Lorraine did seem surprised as well, but since she had seen this place before, she wasn't as shocked as me. I didn't even know who to ask about what. I could at least think of what my first question should be, and maybe I knew who best to ask.

"Was she right about all that?" I asked Gharb and Capitan.

"We wouldn't know what names they have for it outside of our small village," Capitan said, "but we're inside a dungeon within the Lelmudan Empire's territory. That much is certain. That makes Good King Felt our ancestor, apparently. Pretty interesting, eh?"

I suppose it was interesting. Knowing that I had descended from a legendary figure was a bit exciting.

"Why do you assume that?" Lorraine asked them.

"Well, that teleportation circle led here, after all," Gharb said jokingly. But that seemed to actually be their reasoning, so maybe it wasn't a joke.

"The empire found that teleportation circle too, but they couldn't activate it," Lorraine said. "They probably still can't. How did you do it?"

This was the first I'd heard of this, so I asked Lorraine my own question. "They knew about that teleportation circle already?"

"Yes. Unfortunately, this is the sixtieth floor, so even getting this far is a trial. And once you do make it here, you have to deal with the shahor melechnamer and all the other powerful monsters prowling the city. Scholars have tried to investigate it before, but they didn't survive very long, so little progress has ever been made. I know this city by its appearance, and I know of the teleportation circle and how it doesn't work, but that's the extent of my knowledge."

It sounded like they couldn't research the teleportation circle whether they wanted to or not. Maybe I could think of a few ways they could try, but it didn't help that this was also a national secret. That would limit their options for researching it. It was likely a complicated situation.

At any rate, Gharb answered Lorraine's question. "Now, the teleportation circle is similar to the shahor melechnamer in that our blood is the key. That's all there is to it."

"Your blood is the key? I'm not aware of any technology that can do that. Is it similar to how a specific person's mana can be registered to a wand? Maybe you could identify somebody's bloodline similarly," Lorraine murmured to herself. But rather than mull it over, she seemed to think that asking questions would prove more beneficial. "So was I able to use the teleportation circle because I came with Rentt?" she asked Gharb.

"That's absolutely right. I don't know how they did it, but it seems the Ancient Kingdom had technology that made it possible. They could make powerful monsters defend their city, too."

I looked at the gigantic cat lazing about and saw no other explanation aside from what Gharb suggested. But something didn't add up.

"How did such a powerful nation, and a city that inherited that power, get destroyed? And why did their descendants have to go to the outskirts of such a small country?" Lorraine asked, coming to the same conclusion I had.

If they really did have the advanced technology and great power they were purported to have, then they shouldn't have had to leave. Even powerful monsters weren't a threat to them, so I didn't see how they could have been brought to ruin. But to begin with, Good King Felt had fled from some other country and wandered the world until he found his way here.

"It is strange, isn't it?" Gharb said. "I wonder the same thing. And I'm sure the Hatharans who knew about this place before us had the same questions. But we don't have any answers."

"Have you never tried to find out?" I asked. Humans were curious creatures, for better and for worse. Maybe a woman of Gharb's age wasn't going to be quite so interested in her surroundings, but for most people, learning such a big secret would only make you want to find out more. Even if Gharb and Capitan were exceptions to that, there must have been plenty of Hatharans in the past who kept this secret. I found it hard to believe that none of them had ever tried looking deeper.

"It's said that long ago, a few people tried to learn more," Capitan answered. "One such story is only told to the head of the hunters every generation. I think you've got a similar story, right, old lady?"

Gharb nodded. "Yes, a story passed down between what we call medicine women nowadays, but we were once called the chief magician. The mayor once had a different title as well. They used to be called the king."

"If we're bringing that up, then the head hunter used to be called the knight captain, apparently. Considering you can trace the roots of our village back to this place, it makes sense. We're the descendants of a dead country. I don't know if it's worth taking pride in, though. In the end, we're just an ordinary village," Capitan said with a laugh.

After seeing all this, it seemed absurd to call Hathara an ordinary village, but if you looked at it without knowing this secret, it certainly was. I'd always thought so, anyway. All of the villagers aside from these two and my foster father must have seen it that way as well. Once I had left it, I felt like there was something strange about my village, but I didn't think much about it beyond that.

But if they insisted on calling Hathara an ordinary village, why did they bother to bring us here? We could've gone on thinking the village was normal if they hadn't told us about this. The village elders and leaders were supposed to keep this a secret, so this felt unusual.

They said they wanted to unveil this in exchange for asking me something, but this seemed like far too big a secret to reveal.

"Like Capitan just said, Hathara's just an ordinary village now," Gharb said. "Only three of us know the secret anymore, so that's proof enough of that. You see, I thought it'd be best to make it into an ordinary village."

"What do you mean?" I asked.

"I've told you how back in the day, the village was a lot more violent, haven't I? That was because of this place. The chief magician, knight captain, and king are the only roles still left over from the old days, but back when I was young, there was also the chancellor, the minister of justice, and the priest. This was before Capitan or Ingo were even born, back in the previous mayor's day. There were six of us who knew about this city, and we were divided on whether to try and make use of it. The chancellor, minister of justice, and priest asserted that we could use this secret in a way that drew more people to Hathara, expanded the village into a great city, and brought more wealth to the villagers. The other three understood their position, but they weren't eager to approve, from what I heard. After all, this was a secret that had been kept for ages. They didn't want their generation to be the one that exposed it, so that was one reason, but they also feared the potential danger. You can see why, looking at this monster here," Gharb said and petted the shahor melechnamer. It purred like any old cat, but if someone were to actually fight it, it would be deadly. If a small village possessed such strength, somebody would inevitably try to use it. I presumed that was the danger she referred to.

"Were you worried someone outside the village would try to use it?" I asked.

"Yes. There are powerful countries, organizations, and even individuals out there. This monster, this city, and this teleportation circle could all serve as great weapons, but we're simple villagers. There was a strong fear that we would ultimately be taken advantage of and the village would be left to rot. The two sides of this argument never ended up coming to a compromise before it all came to an end."

"How did it end?"

"Well, as I'm sure you've noticed with me and Capitan, everyone with a special role in Hathara inherited special skills. We could all use magic or spirit or the like. These are no ordinary abilities, either. We learned powerful skills passed down since ancient times. The chancellor's side never changed their views, and in the end, they tried to get their way by force. They went up against the opposing side, and the chief magician, knight captain, and king came out victorious. Which is to say the medicine woman, head hunter, and mayor, in today's terms. But there were casualties. The medicine woman was heavily injured, and the head hunter would never hunt again. The mayor fared better, but even he was wounded all over. The chancellor, minister of justice, and priest all died, bringing the conflict to a close."

That was an even bloodier story than I had anticipated. The idea that this village was the site of such a violent battle left me speechless.

Gharb smiled. "Well, that was a long time ago. So, that all happened in an effort to protect this place, when it came down to it. But I was thinking it's time to stop all that. I'm leaving this city in your hands."

"After all the trouble you went through to protect it?"

"Well, the situation has changed. Lorraine here is from the Lelmudan Empire, isn't she? And they know about this place. They found out about it after the conflict in the village, though they still don't seem to know about its connection to Hathara."

Lorraine nodded. "I've heard that the Lelmudan Empire discovered it about fifty years ago, but they haven't found out much. Still, these are ancient ruins, and it's long been said that there must be useful magic items around here. It's been too difficult to explore so far, but trouble has been brewing in the empire as of late. I hear they've reevaluated the significance of these ruins and are proposing new plans to send investigation teams periodically."

"Well, that's the thing," Gharb said. "The chancellor's group said we should reveal the secret after one of them witnessed somebody coming down here. They wanted the glory of unveiling it to the world before somebody else did, I imagine. But many people had come to the city in the past, according to our legends. I thought they only used that sighting as an excuse, but it has turned out to be a problem. If the empire is going to use the full might of their nation to investigate this city, it won't be safe to keep treating it as we always have. I want somebody who's quicker on their feet to watch over it, and you two are just perfect."

"You want us to watch over it?" I said, unsure of how to react. Lorraine looked conflicted as well, as was to be expected. This seemed like a bit much to be leaving in the hands of a couple of people.

Capitan saw what I was thinking. "We're not saying you have to be the only ones to take care of the place, or that we want nothing at all to do with it anymore; nothing like that. It's more that we want some new recruits to the team, you could say." It was like he didn't want it to sound like a demand, but if so, I didn't see why they needed to make this request in the first place.

"Will it not be possible to continue things as you have been?" I asked.

"It could be done, but it'd be nice to have you two join in. There'll be something in it for you, too," Capitan said.

I had no idea what benefit they could offer. Lorraine might appreciate the chance to research the city without having to worry about monsters, but that probably wasn't what he meant.

"Isn't that right, Gharb?" he said, turning to the old woman.

"Yes, well, it'll be easiest to show them. Shall we go have a look?" Gharb said. She climbed onto the shahor melechnamer's back and looked down upon us. "What are you doing? Get on."

Capitan had started to climb on before she'd even said anything. It looked like we would have to ride it. I was a bit reluctant to, but admittedly I'd gotten plenty used to the creature already. Lorraine and I looked at each other and shrugged. Then we got on the shahor melechnamer's back. It was big enough to hold all four of us easily, and it was nice and soft as well. It was so pleasant that I almost wanted to sleep, and I seldom felt sleepy. But if I actually did fall asleep, that would have been a disaster. We were riding this monster somewhere else, so I most likely would have fallen off.

"Now let's go," Gharb said, giving some orders to the shahor melechnamer. It smoothly got into motion, and in a matter of seconds, it reached a frightening speed.

It rushed outside the cave, which is to say into the dungeon city. Ruins of the dead city flew by around us. The cave was on a fairly high wall that let us view the ruins from above. Seeing them up close, the buildings barely looked decayed. It was as if it were a thriving city where the entire population had just vanished. I saw magic lamps glowing in the many buildings, making the empty city look strangely alive.

"Where are we going?!" I shouted.

"Don't look at the city, look at the walls around it!" Gharb shouted back.

I turned to the walls and saw that they were full of holes. They were located at about the same height as the cave we descended from and looked to be the same size too. There were more than I could count.

"I knew it," Lorraine whispered.

"Figured something out?" I asked.

"Yes. You know how I mentioned that the empire found a teleportation circle here?"

"Yeah, but so what?"

"The one they found wasn't in that cave we came from. It was somewhere else. As soon as you descend from the fifty-ninth floor, there's a small cave near the entrance to the city. That's where the one they found is located. Nobody could explore much beyond that due to the monsters."

"So there are multiple teleportation circles?"

"Yes, and possibly more than just those two. All those holes in the walls might contain their own," Lorraine said, trembling a bit.

"That's right!" Gharb yelled. "But I haven't checked all of them, so I couldn't tell you which ones go where!"

"Just thinking about this is terrifying," Lorraine said. "If the empire took control of this city, they would dominate the entire continent."

I nodded. "We can never let them find out. Well, they'd have to be from Hathara to use the teleportation circles, so maybe it'd be fine."

"If anything, I think that would put the people of Hathara in danger," Lorraine added.

It was true that if the people of Hathara themselves were the key, they would likely be targeted. But I couldn't imagine how the empire would reach that conclusion in the first place.

"Speaking of which," Lorraine whispered, remembering something, "Rentt, you were able to use it despite being a vampire. If you brought a vampiric servant along, maybe they could use the teleportation circles too. Vampires create servants by giving another creature some of their blood, after all."

That sounded like an interesting theory, but I would have to try it to know for sure. If only I had brought Edel, but he wasn't with me at the moment. It would be worth attempting in the future though. If it turned out to be possible, then I could single-handedly act as the key for all the teleportation circles. As a consequence, though, I felt like I was now in enormously more danger than ever. If the empire ever figured all this out, they were going to come for me.

We eventually arrived at one of the many caves in the walls, one that was situated far in the back of the city. I thought there would be a teleportation circle here too.

"I don't see anything," I said to Gharb and Capitan. The structure of the cave was identical to the one we were first teleported to. There was a long hallway that led to a big room. It only differed in that nothing was drawn on the ground.

"Well, I'm sure you don't," Gharb said. "But this is the right place. Do it, Capitan."

Capitan took two rocks out of his pocket. One glowed a dull red and one a cloudy blue. He raised the red rock and threw it at the ground with all his might. It split open, and a pattern rapidly materialized on the ground.

"What?! A teleportation circle?" Lorraine exclaimed.

"That's right," Gharb said, nodding. "This is one of the magic items that has been passed down to us. It allows us to create new teleportation circles. The medicine woman and the head hunter receive a pair each. We just used one of them."

"A pair? So the red and blue rocks come as a set?" I asked.

"Yes. It doesn't matter which one you use first, but when you strike one against the ground, it produces a teleportation circle. The exit is created with the other rock. Convenient, eh?" she said.

Not only was it convenient, but if this were put up at an auction, it could sell for an astronomical price. I didn't know about Lorraine, but I'd never seen anything like this before. They wanted to demonstrate how it worked, presumably, but this didn't seem like something to be used lightly.

"You can have this one," Capitan said, handing over the blue rock. "Place the teleportation circle wherever you want."

The rock had looked cloudy from far away, but there were actually tons of tiny glyphs swirling around inside. It looked like a pretty advanced magic item.

"You're giving this to us?" I asked.

"We did say we were letting you look after the city," Capitan said indifferently. "After you get back to Maalt, you don't want to have to take the carriage to Hathara every time you want to visit, right? This'll take you here and back in an instant. Well, it's still half a day's walk between that fortress and Hathara, but it's only a few hours if you hurry. Makes things a lot easier, yeah?"

I appreciated the thought, but I didn't know if I should accept. I looked at Lorraine, who was silently staring at the blue rock, eager to snatch it from my hands. When I handed it to her, she held it right up in front of her eyeballs and gazed into it. She began to mutter about magic theories and such. It was a tiny bit terrifying. But no matter how much success she had as a scholar, obtaining something like this came down to luck, so she was probably exhilarated. I figured it was fine.

"Oh, you can have mine too," Gharb said and gave us her red and blue rocks. "These are still together as a set. Sorry that Capitan went ahead and picked this spot to place one of his."

Hers were a slightly different color than Capitan's, but they looked mostly identical. I had to be careful not to get them confused. The exit, or maybe the entrance if there was any distinction there, being here on this spot was fine by me. According to Gharb, there were plenty more teleportation circles placed here anyway, so we could use these ruins as a hub to easily travel to faraway lands. In fact, even if we had the choice of where to place each teleportation circle, I would have used one here and one in Maalt. I couldn't think of a good place to use the other set, so it was best to hold onto those for the time being. Maybe we would find a vital location for them soon, but we needed to think before we used them.

"Now, would you like to try using some other teleportation circles?" Gharb asked. "I've already checked the destinations of a handful of them."

Lorraine and I nodded.

"All right, then get back on," Gharb said and climbed onto the shahor melechnamer.

We were used to riding it at this point, so we got on more smoothly than before. Once all four of us were settled, the shahor melechnamer got running again.

"I know where this teleportation circle leads, but it's to a bit of a bewildering place. We'll use it first, as usual," Gharb said. Then she and Capitan stood on the teleportation circle and disappeared.

"What do you think she meant by a bewildering place?" I asked Lorraine.

"Maybe a beach next to a stormy sea, or the summit of a volcano."

"Well, I sure hope it's neither of those."

That was a joke, of course, but for something to bewilder someone as brave as Gharb and Capitan, it had to be something of the sort. Waiting behind wasn't an option though, so we stood on the magic circle and warped to an unknown land.

When I got there, I couldn't help but yelp. The first thing I noticed was a fierce stench. Lorraine didn't say anything, but she was wincing. I could see why; the smell was pretty awful.

"See what I mean?" Gharb said with a grin. Capitan was smiling too. This was certainly bewildering.

"So what is this place?" I asked.

"A sewer," Gharb answered. "A secret room inside a sewer, specifically." Gharb felt around the stone wall until part of it slid out of the way with a loud grinding sound. A few seconds later, a path forward appeared, with a waterway on the other side. "Now let's go."

"I wonder if this was here back when that city was thriving," I said as we walked through the sewer.

"It's possible, but probably not," Lorraine said after thinking about it a bit. "Do you know, Gharb?"

Gharb nodded. "Yes, you're correct. This sewer isn't quite so old. It's still old, mind you, but only a few centuries old." The ruined city was presumably thousands of years old, so by comparison, this place didn't have much history.

"But there's a teleportation circle here," I argued. "Those can't be created with modern technology, so it would've had to have been here since the city was active, right?"

"Rentt, have you been paying any attention?" Gharb retorted. "Everyone with a special role in Hathara had a set of those rocks. Some of them used them already, though. This one was left by a chancellor, I believe. A chancellor from long ago."

That made sense, but those people with special roles were supposed to keep the ruins and everything related to them a secret. I didn't understand why they would have made a teleportation circle.

"We're almost to the exit," Gharb said and pointed to some light up ahead. As we got closer, I saw that it wasn't artificial light this time. It came from the sun, and I could see trees outside as if we were in a forest. There was a flowing stream as well.

"Where are we?" I asked. I looked all around me, but I had no idea.

"One moment. *Hide, Rehesteel,*" Gharb chanted. I turned back to the sewer's exit and saw vines and grass grow over it until it was no longer visible.

"That wasn't a spell that Gharb cast," Lorraine said. "Rather, this exit itself is enchanted to react to a magic word. It's very complex, so I don't think it could be canceled easily."

For Lorraine to say that, this must have been fairly advanced magic. An ordinary magician would pass by without even noticing anything, presumably. I was clueless about any of this, though. There was too much to learn about magic. I wanted to be able to talk about the structure of spells and such one day, but maybe that was out of my reach.

We followed Gharb for a while longer. Not that long, but long enough that it felt like a decent walk. Eventually, we saw something.

"Is that a castle? Does that mean we're in the capital?" I asked. There was a massive, towering building before us. Standing in the middle of a city surrounded by high walls, the white building looked majestic and beautiful. There was no structure in this country more grand than this one. We had to be in Vistelya, the capital of the Kingdom of Yaaran. To be honest, I had never been here before. I knew it from books and stories, but this was my first time seeing it in person. Now I knew why the Hatharan villagers got so excited when I talked about Maalt. This was a real city.

I turned to Lorraine to see how she felt, but she looked indifferent. She came from an even bigger city, so maybe this wasn't that special to her, but the difference in her reaction was kind of frustrating. Now I was set on going to the capital of the empire someday.

"Shall we look around a bit before we return?" Gharb said nonchalantly. "There are some materials we were just about to run out of."

"There's somewhere I want to go too," Capitan said. "Let's split up for now and meet back up later."

They sounded much too casual about this. "Are you sure?" I said. "Won't it be strange for Hatharans to just suddenly show up in the capital?"

From what I had heard, Vistelya had gates in the north, south, east, and west, and everyone who came to the city had to prove their identity. Some form of identification had to be presented in order to pass, but I didn't know what they would use.

Just when I was wondering that, they each took out a bronze card that I had seen many times before.

"Aren't those Bronze-class adventurer cards?" I asked. It had been fairly difficult for me to acquire mine the first time, but easy the second time. As to why these two had their own, though, I didn't know.

Capitan seemed to notice why I was staring and answered my question. "We got them for times like these. We used fake names and got them in a city far from Hathara. They won't suspect anything. We do the occasional adventuring work, so there are records of our work history too."

I checked the location of the guild listed on their cards, and it did say the name of a distant city. As far as what jobs they took and how many they did, I would have to work for the guild to check, so I didn't know. Knowing Capitan's skill, it was easy to imagine that he did something impressive. The same went for Gharb. Her card listed a different guild from Capitan's, so they had put a lot of work into the details. They'd probably used the teleportation circles to go pick these up, and it seemed like they used them without much thought. I didn't know if that was the best idea, but on the other hand, these two likely knew to exercise some amount of caution.

"Anyway, go see the sights and enjoy yourselves," Capitan said.

"I'm kind of concerned that we'll look suspicious too," I responded.

"If you use your Rentt Vivie card, you should be fine," Lorraine said.

Maybe that was true. I was supposed to be away from Maalt anyway, so we could say that Rentt Faina was in Hathara while Rentt Vivie was in the capital.

"But what about you, Lorraine?" I asked.

"Me? I have my own method. It's nothing special, but look," Lorraine said and showed me a few different identification cards from the empire. They all featured different names. These were clearly fakes. One of them had her real name, but I doubted she planned to use that. She did things like this sometimes, so I wondered just how Lorraine was treated within the empire, but there was no use asking about that now. Besides, she was who she was, and nothing would change that. It was fine.

"Well, I guess there are no issues, then. Let's go," I said, and we approached the gate to Vistelya.

Afterword

Hello, it's been a while. This is Yu Okano. We've finally reached the sixth book, and I hope we can keep continuing beyond this. It all depends on the support of the readers, so I have to do my best to earn it.

It's strange how things work out. When I first started writing *The Unwanted Undead Adventurer*, I never thought I'd get to turn it into a book, let alone a series that would last this long. I'm sure many of you know this, but these books started as a story I posted to a website where you could share your own novels. This was on an entirely different site from where it's posted now, and under a different title. It was so long ago that my memories are hazy, and I can't even remember exactly what the title was. What I do remember is that I was also writing a novel on the site I'm currently posting to at the same time, but I thought it might be interesting to try writing something somewhere else too. For something that I started from absolutely nothing, though, there was a surprising number of readers. It made me feel like more people were interested in my writing than I thought, so I figured it might be best to move the story to the site that had more users overall. I've since completely stopped posting to the original site, and my account isn't even there anymore, but sometimes I wonder if there's anyone who's kept up with the story since all the way back then. There weren't even twenty readers at the time, I don't think. If any of you are out there, please contact me.

Anyway, after many twists and turns, the story came to be published as a series of books. I'm very attached to this story, and as I'm writing it, I feel like I'd love to keep it going forever. But all stories have to end one day. If you'd keep reading until that day comes, nothing would make me happier as an author. Please stick around for more *The Unwanted Undead Adventurer*.

7

author
u Okano

llustrator
aian

he Unwanted Undead Adventurer

NOVEL Volume 7: On Sale August 2022

MANGA Volume 6: On Sale July 2022

Author:
616th Special Information Battalion
Volume 4
On Sale
August 2022!
Her Majesty's Swarm
vol. 4

HEY///////
▶ **HAVE YOU HEARD OF**
J-Novel Club?

It's the digital publishing company that brings you the latest novels from Japan!

Subscribe today at

▶ ▶ ▶**j-novel.club**◀ ◀ ◀

and read the latest volumes as they're translated, or become a premium member to get a *FREE* ebook every month!

━━ Check Out The Latest Volume Of ━━

The Unwanted Undead Adventurer

Plus Our Other Hit Series Like:

▶ Black Summoner
▶ John Sinclair: Demon Hunter
▶ Otherside Picnic
▶ Her Majesty's Swarm
▶ The Faraway Paladin
▶ Altina the Sword Princess
▶ Demon Lord, Retry!
▶ Seirei Gensouki: Spirit Chronicles

　　...and many more!

▶ Slayers
▶ Arifureta: From Commonplace to World's Strongest
▶ Der Werwolf: The Annals of Veight
▶ How a Realist Hero Rebuilt the Kingdom
▶ By the Grace of the Gods
▶ Lazy Dungeon Master
▶ Dungeon Busters
▶ An Archdemon's Dilemma: How to Love Your Elf Bride

In Another World With My Smartphone, Illustration © Eiji Usatsuka　　*Arifureta: From Commonplace to World's Strongest*, Illustration © Takayaki

J-Novel Club Lineup

Latest Ebook Releases Series List

Altina the Sword Princess
Amagi Brilliant Park
Animeta!**
The Apothecary Diaries
An Archdemon's Dilemma: How to Love Your Elf Bride*
Are You Okay With a Slightly Older Girlfriend?
Arifureta: From Commonplace to World's Strongest
Arifureta Zero
Ascendance of a Bookworm*
Banner of the Stars
Bibliophile Princess*
Black Summoner*
The Bloodline
By the Grace of the Gods
Campfire Cooking in Another World with My Absurd Skill*
Can Someone Please Explain What's Going On?!
Chillin' in Another World with Level 2 Super Cheat Powers
The Combat Baker and Automaton Waitress
Cooking with Wild Game*
Culinary Chronicles of the Court Flower
Dahlia in Bloom: Crafting a Fresh Start with Magical Tools
Deathbound Duke's Daughter
Demon Lord, Retry!*
Der Werwolf: The Annals of Veight*
Dragon Daddy Diaries: A Girl Grows to Greatness
Dungeon Busters
The Emperor's Lady-in-Waiting Is Wanted as a Bride*
Endo and Kobayashi Live! The Latest on Tsundere Villainess Lieselotte
The Faraway Paladin*
Full Metal Panic!
Full Clearing Another World under a Goddess with Zero Believers*
Fushi no Kami: Rebuilding Civilization Starts With a Village
Goodbye Otherworld, See You Tomorrow
The Great Cleric
The Greatest Magicmaster's Retirement Plan

Girls Kingdom
Grimgar of Fantasy and Ash
Hell Mode
Her Majesty's Swarm
Holmes of Kyoto
How a Realist Hero Rebuilt the Kingdom*
How NOT to Summon a Demon Lord
I Shall Survive Using Potions!*
I'll Never Set Foot in That House Again!
The Ideal Sponger Life
If It's for My Daughter, I'd Even Defeat a Demon Lord
In Another World With My Smartphone
Infinite Dendrogram*
Invaders of the Rokujouma!?
Jessica Bannister
JK Haru is a Sex Worker in Another World
John Sinclair: Demon Hunter
A Late-Start Tamer's Laid-Back Life
Lazy Dungeon Master
A Lily Blooms in Another World
Maddrax
The Magic in this Other World is Too Far Behind!*
The Magician Who Rose From Failure
Mapping: The Trash-Tier Skill That Got Me Into a Top-Tier Party*
Marginal Operation**
The Master of Ragnarok & Blesser of Einherjar*
Min-Maxing My TRPG Build in Another World
Monster Tamer
My Daughter Left the Nest and Returned an S-Rank Adventurer
My Friend's Little Sister Has It In for Me!
My Instant Death Ability is So Overpowered, No One in This Other World Stands a Chance Against Me!*
My Next Life as a Villainess: All Routes Lead to Doom!
Otherside Picnic
Outbreak Company
Perry Rhodan NEO

Private Tutor to the Duke's Daughter
Reborn to Master the Blade: From Hero-King to Extraordinary Squire ♀*
Record of Wortenia War*
Reincarnated as the Piggy Duke: This Time I'm Gonna Tell Her How I Feel!
The Reincarnated Princess Spends Another Day Skipping Story Routes
Seirei Gensouki: Spirit Chronicles*
Sexiled: My Sexist Party Leader Kicked Me Out, So I Teamed Up With a Mythical Sorceress!
She's the Cutest... But We're Just Friends!
The Sidekick Never Gets the Girl, Let Alone the Protag's Sister!
Slayers
The Sorcerer's Receptionist
Sorcerous Stabber Orphen*
Sweet Reincarnation**
The Tales of Marielle Clarac*
Tearmoon Empire
Teogonia
The Underdog of the Eight Great Tribes
The Unwanted Undead Adventurer*
Villainess: Reloaded! Blowing Away Bad Ends with Modern Weapons*
Welcome to Japan, Ms. Elf!*
The White Cat's Revenge as Plotted from the Dragon King's Lap
A Wild Last Boss Appeared!
The World's Least Interesting Master Swordsman

...and more!
* Novel and Manga Editions
** Manga Only
Keep an eye out at j-novel.club for further new title announcements!